LIVING THE LEGEND

THE IAN FRANCIS STORY

MARYANNE LEIGHTON

LIVING THE LEGEND
THE IAN FRANCIS STORY

Published by
Quarter Horse Australia
A division of the Australian Quarter Horse Association
131 Gunnedah Road
PO Box 979
Tamworth NSW 2340
Phone: 02 6762 6444
ABN 41 000 964 643

Design
Jenna Bignell

Typography and Production
Australian Quarter Horse Magazine

Cover Photo
One Hellofa Spin Q-42160. Courtesy: Dave Christensen

Printing
Kudos Colour Printing
Kedron, Queensland.

First Edition: June 2007

ISBN 978 0 646 47563 9

I am grateful to the many people who helped me with this book, most especially to Ian whose story this is. Thank you for laying bare your soul and allowing me access to the hidden corners of your life – you are a brave man and it has been a joy working with you.

Thanks to Hunter Jones for having the courage to accept my challenge, to Tara Gordon and Jenna Bignell who always make me look good in print, to Virginia Lemon for your hospitality, to all Ian's friends (almost without exception his clients become his friends) and family who generously shared their memories of him, and to my daughter, Virginia, who is my writing buddy, sounding board, proof reader and number one research assistant.

*Quotes in left hand margins are taken from 'That Winning Attitude"
by Ian Francis*

*MaryAnne Leighton
June 2007*

FOREWARD

All of my life I have had a burning desire to be around horses. Everything about them engages my mind – from the way they smell to the interaction between a horse and a trainer. My craving for knowledge about how to get the best out of each horse I possibly can has always been endless. Even at an early age I was drawn to great horsemen. I would listen, watch and ask a million questions about their training techniques. I was lucky enough to live in an area that I was able to see Ian Francis at horse shows, and I was immediately attracted to what he could do with a horse. He clearly was above and beyond his fellow competitors, and he always made everything look so easy. From the first time I saw Ian on a horse, I knew he was the one I wanted to emulate during my career.

I am one of the lucky ones that had the opportunity to work for Ian. The knowledge he imparted to me is irreplaceable. Every day I draw on the deep well of techniques I have learned from Ian. Isn't it funny though that so often we never want what is in our own backyard until it's gone or we have seen the other side of things? I always knew Ian was a great horseman, but in my youthful ignorance, I thought surely in my quest for knowledge I would find a horseman even more talented than Ian. It wasn't until several years later, with age, experience and travels halfway around the world that I came to realize I would never find anyone better than Ian Francis. He was, is, and continues to be what I consider the best horseman in the world.

You might say to yourself "best in the world? That's a pretty bold statement." Well, yes it is, but no one deserves that bold statement more than Ian Francis. I've spent the last ten years of my life in the US, and I've studied with every great reining, cow horse and cutting trainer in the country. I will admit for a few brief years, I thought these "World Champion" trainers had to be better than Ian. Why? Because everyone in Australia always thinks the US has better horses, better trainers, and just a higher caliber horse culture in general. Well, let me tell you, I have seen all there is to see here in the States and there is no mistaking there are some legendary trainers here, but I still say that Ian is the best in the world. He has more feel and timing in his little toe than most trainers (even legends and world champions) have in their entire bodies

To this day, I invite Ian over to my ranch here in the States for a week every year so I can keep learning from the master and improving my own skills under his tutelage. Ian can make a horse with the most average abilities do things that make you go "wow" and I always learn something new from our time spent together, even after all these years. One thing is for sure, don't ever mistake Ian Francis for anything but a master – if you underestimate him, he's sure to pass you by and you'll never know where he came from.

There will never be another Ian Francis!

Clinton R. Anderson
Trainer and Clinician

February 2007

PROLOGUE

When I was first approached about this book I was apprehensive. Being portrayed as a legend makes me uncomfortable because that is not the image I have of myself. When I look at the record of achievement we created - and I say we because I sure didn't get this all done by myself, most of the time I had great support - the record is remarkable. It makes me think of the fellow down at the bar who has run brumbies, thrown bulls, hunted crocodiles, charmed snakes and caught whales on a hand-line and when you work it out he would had to have lived three hundred years to have achieved it all. But we did get this done and when I look at it I think that I have the right to feel a bit arthritic and more than a bit tired and worn some days.

I am so fortunate to have a great network of people I can turn to for advice and support. I would love to name them all and give them credit but I know that as soon as this goes to print I would remember someone else who deserves mention. These are all quality people in my view; they give support to my ambitions but have the strength of character to tell me if they feel I have done the wrong thing or are heading in the wrong direction. I hope you can take some pride and pleasure from the part you played in my success.

What is this story about? It is about success born out of humble beginnings. It is about success hampered by love expectations and low self esteem. It is about changing your attitude so you can change your life. It is about being handicapped by injury and still going on. It is about knowing that when you ride out in a final and the money's up that all of this doesn't matter; the other competitors aren't going to give you any advantage and the judges and spectators don't care, they are just looking for a winner. Or at least I think that's what it is about.

Ian Francis
Windera, Queensland
March 2007

CONTENTS

CHAPTER 1 - THE LEGEND BEGINS

'TO CHANGE YOUR
LIFE YOU MUST
FIRST CHANGE
YOUR ATTITUDE.'

Ian Francis's earliest and most enduring memories are of his yearning for a horse. Every birthday he asked for a horse, every Christmas he asked for a horse and every year he watched those important days pass without receiving the only gift he ever wanted, receiving school books and additions to his school uniform instead. Thoughts of horses consumed his childhood but Ian was born at the conclusion of World War II, in the decade following the Great Depression and there was no money for something so frivolous as a horse even if his parents had the inclination to buy one for him. They could not understand his obsession and would not discuss it, believing it would pass as most childhood obsessions do. Ian's parents were wrong. His passion for horses has never waned and remains as strong today as it was when he was a child.

Ian was born on 28 June 1945 in the thriving coastal Queensland town of Maryborough, the eldest of Snow and Ella Francis's three chil-

dren. Ian's father was a gentle, quiet man of few words but a keen sense of humour which he has passed to Ian. Although Snow never discussed his own childhood Ian knew his father resented the fact that his own parents had separated when he was a child and that he was raised by his grandmother on a small farm near the remote country town of Gayndah. Ian's mother, Ella, was a severe woman who was Scottish-born and arrived in Australia as a toddler. Ian never knew any of his grandparents and he feels the lack of an extended family, of not knowing his family's history and where he came from. Snow was a farm worker until World War II broke out, then he drove trucks and cut timber before taking up an apprenticeship as a carpenter, eventually working as a maintenance carpenter at Walker Shipyards in Maryborough. Wages in the 1940s were low and Snow and Ella, with their young family, moved frequently, often sharing houses with other families because they could not afford to rent an entire home of their own. Eventually Snow used his carpentry skills to build a tiny, two-bedroom fibro house on a quarter acre section in Hyne Street, Maryborough. Snow intended to build a third bedroom for Ian but never got further than putting posts in the ground for the frame so, from when he was a child until he left home to get married at the age of eighteen, Ian slept on a sofa in the lounge and kept his clothes in his parents' bedroom. The family's sturdy, well-built home remains unchanged today and is now owned by Ian's cousin.

The Francis family did not own a car but Snow had a pushbike and Ian remembers when he was about four, standing on the bar of the bike with his arm around Snow's neck and his little suitcase strapped to a carrier on the back as his father took him to hospital to have his tonsils removed. Snow's watering hole in the late 1940s was The Carrier's Arms Hotel where the bar consisted of a long bench on which sat beer kegs that were covered with wet sacks to keep the beer cool. The menfolk in the Francis family have been blessed with a gene that causes early hair loss. In describing his baldness, Snow called himself an eggshell blonde in reference to the 1930s Hollywood movie star, Jean Harlow, who was known as the blonde bombshell. Snow kindly passed on his early hair-loss gene to Ian along with his sense of the ridiculous.

Although the family had very little money, Ian describes a happy childhood of fishing for shrimps, picking guavas and playing in the moonlight, of telling jokes and playing practical jokes. He, his sister, Kay, and their friends slid down hills on chunks of cardboard and made boats from roofing iron that they knew would sink as soon as they were launched. Ian was a good cricket player and gained his early skills when he, Kay and their friends set up wickets down the middle of Hyne Street and he was the ringleader of a tribe of kids who regularly 'borrowed' vegetables from a market garden one kilometre from home. Kay discovered thirty years later that they were not as clever as they had thought; the market gardener sat at the top of the hill and watched them raid his crops but he never worried because they caused no damage and only took what they needed. This was a childhood of freedom and safety, of doors left unlocked and of kids riding their pushbikes for miles, not coming home until the day was ended and night set in. Kay says she and Ian had to be home by five o'clock each evening and, being typical kids, at the end of every day they left it until the last minute to jump the fence and run inside minutes before their father arrived home from work.

Ian laments his family's total lack of interest in animals of any description, especially horses and cattle. He says, 'Any interest my family had in livestock existed only in my mind.' He was a skinny, intense kid whose obsession with any cow that wandered past and every horse that ever existed drove his parents to distraction. Apart from playing sport, every spare moment he ever had, every afternoon after school, every weekend and every public holiday, he made himself terribly useful to anyone in the district who owned livestock, just so he could be around the animals. He was eleven when he first rode a horse, an old brumby that belonged

Ian's parents, Ella & Snow Francis

Ian and his sisters, Kay (left) and Diana

Ian's great-uncle, Joe Atkinson (left), champion Australian rodeo rider in the 1920s from whom Ian believes he inherited his horsemanship skills.

'I'M NOT WORTHY OF SADDLING HIS HORSE – HE'S IN A CLASS ALL OF HIS OWN.'
BARRY WHITAKER, MENTOR AND FRIEND OF OVER 50 YEARS

'ONLY THOSE WHO RISK GOING TOO FAR, CAN POSSIBLY FIND HOW FAR THEY CAN GO.'

Photo: Don Davies Photographer, Maryborough

Ian aged 13 (left) and Stewart Whitaker leading a bullock team in the 1958 Mary Khana Procession, patriarch Sam Whitaker on right. Ian is probably the only trainer working today who can say he often helped a real bullocky to yoke-up his team. Ian was not wearing a hat because he did not own one.

Barry Whitaker (left) and Ian cutting posts for fencing - by now Ian could afford a hat

to a nearby dairy farmer for whom he worked after school. Ian did all the dirty work on the farm just so he could ride the old horse to bring the cows in for milking then take them back out to their paddock when the milking was done. Sometimes during the winter he was allowed to take the cows to Ilulu Park which now forms part of the Maryborough Golf Course. There Ian taught himself to ride and 'trained' the horse while the cows grazed between the tennis and netball courts until it was time to take them home for the next milking. Although the farmer owned milking machines he did not like using them so Ian sat under the machines and happily milked eight cows an hour by hand, dreaming of his next ride on the brumby or figuring out where he could borrow another horse or scrounge another ride.

Ian and his young friends, Alan Heath, Judy Harley and Barry and Trevor Keene, fancied themselves as rodeo riders but they needed stock to develop their rodeo skills. The enterprising thirteen-year-olds convinced a local dairy farmer that he needed a set of yards

'just in case' his cows needed to be sprayed. Or something. They built a set of yards in the shape of an hourglass – two circles connected by a crush. 'We never had gates so we used to put four rails in front of an old dairy cow and slip one behind her. We'd have to get a rope on her and put our feet up on her neck so we didn't rip our knees off on the posts coming out, then we'd have to put them down pretty quick and we'd buck the cows out one way then run them back in and buck them out the other way.' The lack of a proper saddle bronc to practice on was no problem to these inventive kids who simply saddled up a cow. Those old Guernsey cows had prominent backbones and the saddle was not a good fit. Also, unlike a horse, a cow has the ability to bend its tail over its back so putting the crupper on to hold the saddle in place was a waste of time – as soon as the cow bucked the saddle and rider immediately flew off over its head. If Les Heath ever knew what those kids were up to with his dry cows, he never let on.

One of Ian's great school friends was Stewart Whitaker whose family lived on the outskirts of Maryborough. The Whitaker family had cattle – and they had horses. Stewart and his brothers Barry, Winston and John were known to be capable bush men and good horsemen and Ian virtually lived with them from the time he was twelve until he married at the age of eighteen. Together the young men felled trees, cut fence posts and rails, cut house stumps, sapped poles for the Public Works Department, chased roos, learned about cattle and horses and at smoko acted like bushies, slurping tea out of the one billy can. Barry says Ian has always worked hard, even when he was a young kid, often working for no pay. Ian credits Barry Whitaker with sparking his interest in a higher level of horsemanship and he was the first person Ian met who made him think of using horses for more than just transport. Although Barry was not an educated horseman he had a natural ability, wonderful balance, was exceptionally good with young horses and Ian learned a lot from him. Talking about Ian, Barry said, 'I didn't teach Franko to ride, he just thieved ideas from me!' When Ian was sixteen he was able to buy his first horse, fulfilling his life's dream. Barry Whitaker owned an exotic-looking gelding whose father was a pony and his mother a draft mare and he sold Ed to Ian for £3, exactly one week's wage. Ed was a medium-sized horse with huge feet, an even bigger head and he loved to buck, but to Ian he was perfect - until the day he nearly killed Ian. Out riding with Winston and Stewart, Ed fell and Ian's spur became tangled in the old cord girth. Ed bolted down the track, kicking at Ian and connecting every time. After what felt like miles but was only thirty or forty feet, the cord broke. Full of bravado, Ian leapt to his feet saying, 'I'm fine, I'm fine, catch my horse,' then collapsed, shaking as shock hit him. Ed soon found a new home.

In the 1950s a career involving horses – other than as a racehorse trainer - did not exist. Ian's parents were adamant that there was no money in horses and no future in them so Ian always believed his career would revolve around cattle. He started school at the age of five, a year younger than his classmates. He was a good student and passed all his exams until he turned fourteen when algebra and chemistry reared their ugly heads and caused him to struggle with his studies for the first time. He begged to leave school but, like every parent of their time, Snow and Ella craved security following the Great Depression and their aim was for their son to get a good education followed by a 'safe' job with the government. Eventually they agreed he could leave school on the condition that he applied for a Government job. While the fourteen-year-old Ian waited for this suitable job to appear, Snow arranged a temporary employment for him at Coburn and Watson's Foundry in Maryborough. Ian said, 'This was a tough place to work; anyone who found it hard to get a job anywhere else could always find work at the foundry and many of the staff had prison records, some were old ex-fighters and others were alcoholics.' Snow instructed the foundry's owner to 'work Ian to death' for six weeks in the hope that it would encourage him to go back to school. As a deterrent to leaving school this job was a dismal failure but it probably contributed to the strong work ethic that Ian retains to this day. He survived six months at the foundry then, to his horror, was offered a

1962 cutting cane at Bidwill

Ian and Beryl Francis

Part of the shunting yards at Maryborough Railway Centre

Photo: John Hall 'The Queenslander'

safe Government job as a trainee station master for the Maryborough Railway. Ian started at the bottom as a porter, alongside his friend, Barry Whitaker, for a weekly wage of £3. To put this into perspective, a pair of coveted R.M. Williams boots cost £10, more than three weeks' wages. Barry remembers watching Ian working the levers that controlled the tracks in the shunting yard. He said, 'There were something like fifty-four levers in the cabin and Ian worked the whole lot without making a mistake or getting confused. It was like watching a dance and at the age of sixteen he really did all the work of the station master.' After three long years, at the age of seventeen, he quit this safe job to go

'HE'S A VERY HONEST PERSON. I DON'T THINK HE WOULD RIP OFF THE TAX MAN IF HE HAD THE OPPORTUNITY.'
BERYL FRANCIS (JENSEN)

'IAN IS ALWAYS SUCH A FUN PERSON TO BE AROUND.'
SANDY STASSEN, CLIENT AND FRIEND

'I ONCE SAID TO IAN THAT I COULD NEVER DO WITH HORSES WHAT HE DOES AND HE REPLIED THAT MAYBE I DIDN'T WANT TO.'
BARRY WHITAKER, MENTOR AND FRIEND OF MORE THAN 50 YEARS

'IF YOU HAD THE
POWER TO CHANGE
SOMETHING AND
DIDN'T, YOU DON'T
HAVE THE RIGHT
TO COMPLAIN
ABOUT IT.'

Beryl gave Ian this grey mare for his 21st birthday. He celebrated his 21st by building pig pens and they celebrated Beryl's 21st by planting grain crops in the rain. Ian broke in this mare and was sacked from his job when he objected to the boss riding her in his absence.

Showing the Champion Poll Hereford bull at Rockhampton 1970

Ian (centre) at a veterinary training seminar where he learned how to remove eye cancers and castrate bull calves

Getting the timber for yards at Harrami

1962 riding Abattoir Special

Loading cane at Childers 1964

14

fencing and cut sugar cane – anything to be out of town and back in his beloved bush.

In 1962 Ian moved to Childers where he spent one season cutting sugar cane by knife. There was little time for levity and no time for reflection in the cane fields but he remembers frequently roaring with laughter as blue mountain parrots feasted and got drunk on fermented sugar, turning somersaults and falling off the cane in their drunken stupor. Towards the end of the season with only a little cane remaining to be cut Ian saw his very first mechanical sugar cane harvester. He said, 'The mill was closing at the end of the season and they brought in a harvester to help us finish up. The harvesters really took over the industry very quickly and after that the only cane that was cut by knife was the sets cut for planting.' Ian returned to Maryborough where he earned a living fencing and where he met Beryl Jensen, a farmer's daughter from Bidwill. Ian and Beryl married in 1964 when Ian was eighteen and Beryl sixteen and for the first six months of their married life they lived with Beryl's parents while Ian cut cane for her father, Eric. In January 1965 they accepted a position on a property at Coominglah, near Monto in Queensland. Ian had decided to only take jobs that allowed him to use his own horses which he broke and trained while carrying out farm work. This thousand acre property which ran cattle and grew small crops, wheat and oats was an ideal set-up for training his horses and Ian ran the property single-handed with only Beryl to help. The young couple was happy, they did everything together, went everywhere together and Beryl said they never needed a radio in the truck as Ian always sang when he drove. Unfortunately he has an appalling singing voice. He says, 'No one told me I couldn't sing - poor Beryl had to put up with me making a terrible noise for twenty years!' Beryl loved the property at Coominglah but she describes the house they lived in as 'pretty primitive'. There was one tap outside, another in the downstairs laundry/bathroom and water had to be carried upstairs until Ian installed a small water tank on a stand giving them water in the kitchen. Beryl cooked on an old wood stove for which she chopped wood with a blunt axe, electricity in the house was courtesy of a 32 volt battery

system and the seals in the door of the kerosene fridge had long perished giving blowflies unrestricted access to the meat inside.

After two happy years at Coominglah, Ian and Beryl moved to a nearby cattle property. Their neighbour, Henry Surtees, describes the house they lived in for the next year as 'not suitable for a pig'. It was tumbledown, had tar paper on the walls, an old wood stove and a 12 volt electric system which was so out-of-date it was almost impossible to find appliances to use with it. Henry remembers Ian and Beryl working from five in the morning until after dark and, because the dilapidated farm vehicle had no lights, Beryl was forced to sit on the bonnet with a torch in her hand to light their way home. Henry says he has never known two people to have so little for so long. He remembers Ian once asking Beryl if they had enough money for him to enter a bull ride at Dawes Rodeo. The answer was yes and his winnings added to the little money they had. After working in this hostile environment for twelve months, a chance meeting with Henry resulted in Ian and Beryl moving in 1968 to a good scrub property, La Terre Riante (The Smiling Land) at Harrami, thirty-six miles from Monto. Ian was employed as overseer on the Poll Hereford stud, a position he enjoyed for another two years.

Ian dabbled in boxing and rodeo riding in his teens and early twenties but they were activities he did not pursue seriously. He remembers once fighting the Queensland Lightweight Champion, Trevor Hawkins, a boxer who had had ten knockouts in a row. 'On the night I could have and should have beaten him but I didn't because I didn't expect to. I was the first guy ever to go the distance with him but he beat me by one point. He never hurt me and I remember thinking later that I should have won that.' Ian also regrets that he did not take his rodeo career more seriously and did not put more effort into it. He said, 'I hate to blame my upbringing but as a child I wasn't expected to aspire to be good at anything. I was never pushed to excel, never encouraged to be a winner and I didn't understand that I could expect better of myself.' Ian was insecure and had no self confidence. He says, 'I was too introverted

'JUST BECAUSE HE HAS HORSE SKILLS DOESN'T MEAN HE HAS MECHANICAL HORSE SKILLS. MY SON, JASON, KNEW HE WAS AT THE RIGHT PLACE WHEN HE CALLED IN TO WINDERA. THERE WAS THE TRACTOR, BROKEN DOWN IN THE MIDDLE OF THE PADDOCK, SAME AS AT WIDGEE!'
NORMA WHITLEY, FRIEND OF MORE THAN 40 YEARS

'IAN'S SINGING ABILITY COULD BE COMPARED TO HIS ABILITY TO SWING A ROPE!'
KEN MAY, CLINICIAN, MENTOR AND FRIEND OF MORE THAN 30 YEARS

'ALL THE ADVICE IN THE WORLD IS NOT MUCH HELP, IF YOU DON'T ACT ON IT.'

Campdrafting at Teebar in the 1970s

Stud cattle open day at Harrami

and I had a perception of inferiority that lasted a long time and affected my approach to boxing and rodeo. I would never approach someone like Chilla Seeney for example and ask him to teach me how to ride a saddle bronc and I regret that I didn't do anywhere near as good as I now know I could have done.'

Ian's attitudes were formed at home, at school and in his social environment. He recalls when he was thirteen his teacher asked what he wanted to be when he left school. Ian's response was that he wanted to raise beef cattle and he was mightily offended by the teacher's dismissive response. Sam Whitaker, father of Ian's friends Stewart and Barry, was described by Ian as a cantankerous man of few words. Sam also asked Ian what he wanted to do with his life and when Ian replied that he would like to have a property one day, but he doubted he would have enough to buy a burial plot, Sam's response was, 'You think you will have that much?' Many years later, Stewart commented that his father probably did Ian a favour with that hurtful comment; he got Ian out of bed every day for the rest of his life, just to prove him wrong. In 1968 Ian retired from rodeo competition and was nominated to the judging panel of the South East Queensland Rodeo Association where he served as a qualified rodeo judge for the next twelve years, until increasing commitments forced his retirement. During that time he competed extensively in campdrafting, always riding young horses that he had broken in and trained but none of which he managed to keep beyond its first few wins as his horses were always in demand by other campdrafters who took them on to greater things.

Ian describes how his lack of confidence in his horsemanship and his perception of his own inferiority changed when he went to work for John Kingston and began showing horses for clients. John Kingston was a Maryborough businessman, a pharmacist, veterinary surgeon and the principal of Kingston Rural Management. KRM managed a number of large properties for absentee owners and in 1971 John offered Ian a position as on-site property manager at Spanjur, adjacent to Ian's in-laws' farm at Bidwill. Ian was the first KRM on-site manager who was not college educated and initially John was reluctant to offer him the job, partly because of his lack of a tertiary education but also because of his association with the Whitaker brothers whom he regarded as rogues. Although John says Ian fitted into the company well, Kingston Rural Management was a revelation to Ian. Suddenly this boy from the bush was presented with management meetings, budgets, scientific monitoring of cattle and John's weekly newsletters. 'I came to call those things poison pen letters; they contained information on every damn thing to do with the rural sector. All the managers got them and when I left after two years I had a removal van full of the stuff.' Ian still has a few of those poison pen letters today.

John Kingston was a motivator and was instrumental in Ian's change of attitude and change of focus. 'Suddenly I was working for people who had expectations and set goals and I found I was achieving things that were way above my expectations of myself. So I stopped having expectations and thought I'd just go up the hill and see where it leads. I haven't found the top of the hill yet.' Ian's neighbour, Rob Irvine, was thirty-six, had $600 in the bank and announced that he would retire when he turned forty-six

Ian and Danny

Danny with O'Donnell the Poll Hereford bull 1974

- and he did. He encouraged Ian to focus his attention on the things he wanted to achieve and gave him a motivational tape and this, combined with John Kingston introducing him to motivational books, further inspired Ian and helped his thinking. The second-most important thing that came out of Ian's association with John Kingston was his awareness of how critical it is for a successful horse trainer to also be a successful businessman and in the late 1970s he began planning for his future by acquiring business skills. John says, 'The horse industry is a most unbusinesslike environment. It is not a hatching ground for smart businessmen and it was not easy for Ian to develop business skills.' It may not have been easy but he did it while at the same time developing a comprehensive knowledge of bulldozer clearing, sub-tropical pasture development and cattle cross-breeding using artificial insemination, while increasing his fencing and yard-building skills and conducting the horse-handling and riding section of training schools run by Kingston Rural Management.

Ian became a goal-seeker and one early, compelling goal was to accumulate assets of one million dollars, through his own efforts and hard work. It took him twenty-five years but he achieved that goal and every other goal he set himself throughout his life.

In 1972 Tommy Roche, the owner of La Terre Riante, died and as his heirs knew nothing about stud cattle they asked Ian to return. This was a milestone as he was able to buy a share in the property and ran it as part-owner and manager, realising another of his childhood dreams. These were good days, Ian was increasingly in demand for his horse training skills and he frequently held shows at Harrami, a major drawcard at these shows being Chilla Seeney with his magnificent cutting stallion, Mr Jessie James*. His friends, Len and Norma Whitley, had introduced him to Quarter Horses and in 1974 they loaned him a mare so he could breed his first Quarter Horse foal, a chestnut filly he named Cool Charm and sold through Rocky Sale.

In 1973, Ian and Beryl were ecstatic with the arrival of their first child when they adopted three-week-old Danny and in 1977 they completed their family when they adopted six-week-old Kris Ann. The kids were a delight. As Danny grew he followed his father everywhere, always seeking dad's approval. Norma Whitley remembers the young Danny's favourite game was swinging from the light cord and landing on his bed and there were plenty of the usual childhood dramas like Danny contracting chicken pox on one of the few family holidays at the beach and falling from the grandstand and hitting his head at a show. Krissie was less accident-prone but when she choked on a twenty cent piece, she did it in style. Krissie shares her father's love of wildlife and birds. Ian had hom-

'IAN WAS ALWAYS GOING TO BE A SUCCESS, WHATEVER HE TOOK ON.'
LAWRIE HEADING, MENTOR AND FRIEND OF 40 YEARS

'HE'S A GOOD MAN.'
KRIS ANN FRANCIS

'IAN HAS NEVER TRIED TO BE ANYONE ELSE. HE ALWAYS LOOKED FOR HIS OWN HORIZON.'
NORMA WHITLEY, FRIEND OF MORE THAN 40 YEARS

'SOME THINGS
DON'T DESERVE
THE WORRY WE
GIVE THEM.'

Ian aged 31 with eight-week-old Kris Ann and three-year-old Danny, 1976

ing pigeons when he was a child and the kitchen of the little house at Widgee had a one-way window through which the family could watch native birds eating at the bird feeder that Ian installed. While he prefers to see birds in the wild, Krissie is a licensed breeder of exotic parrots. Danny, who recently presented Ian and Beryl with their first grandchild, little Danno, has had a variety of interesting jobs ranging from stained glass restoration to catering and farm work and now works in the national gas industry.

In the mid-1970s the cattle industry was hit by a downturn and prices plummeted. Ian's concern about the viability of remaining at Harrami was alleviated when John Kingston asked him to take over as manager, property developer and horse trainer at Kolora Quarter Horse Stud at Maryborough. Ian says that while he wore the label of manager, in reality John was the manager and he just did the work, the very hard work of managing two stallions and forty-six broodmares on two hundred acres of gently undulating land on the banks of the Mary River while

With Kolora Stud's mare, Angelique, at Kolora

building yards, fences and the infrastructure necessary to run a working stud and training facility. John Kingston says, 'It was a hell of a hard job but Ian is a hard worker – he had to be to work for us.' Jenny Kingston agrees but adds, 'Ian had no self confidence and absolutely no idea of his own abilities as a horseman. I once watched him at a show hitting the boot of the car in anger and frustration because he couldn't bring himself to ride a horse in the arena and compete. He could show at halter but that was as far as he could go. I suspect he knew he could be competitive but his mind and conditioning were an impenetrable barrier.' She says, 'The turning point for Ian came when he was in his early thirties and we sent him to a John Stanton school where everyone had to do a campdraft run to show how much they knew. After Ian's run, John Stanton told him there was nothing he could teach him and predicted he would become a great horseman. Ian came home a changed man; the difference in his outlook and confidence was amazing.'

Ian always acknowledges the changes that John Stanton brought to his attitude at that one brief school and in reply John Stanton says, 'I never had anyone who could catch on quicker than Ian Francis. He is so talented and so gifted in so many ways and he has a tremendous ability to show a horse what he wants. How do you explain to someone who doesn't have that gift?' Instead of breaking for lunch with the other attendees, Ian followed John to watch him train a dog and spent every lunch time asking questions about horses. When he returned from that school Ian began showing horses in western performance classes and after his two-year contract at Kolora expired he returned to Harrami, training and showing the Kingstons' horses and preparing others for Rockhampton Quarter Horse sale. He quickly established a reputation as a trainer to watch out for and his success at a show in 1980 caused judge and successful Quarter Horse breeder and competitor, Lyn Uhlman, to exclaim, 'Where the hell did that guy come from?' Jenny Kingston says, 'The transformation in Ian took him to the other extreme and he is now able to compete under the most extreme pressure. He is virtually unbeatable in a run-off.'

With Kings Gold at Biloela Ag Show 1980

The first Quarter Horse Ian ever owned was Kings Gold, a horse he still rates very highly. Ian said, 'Kings Gold was the first really significant show horse in my life. Jenny Kingston bred him and she and John offered me a deal to start him, show him if he had any talent or to sell him on if he didn't work out. He turned out great in spite of my efforts to screw him up. Chilla Seeney remarked that I made the horse four times and messed him up five times. I showed him in just about every event; halter, trail, western riding, cow horse, cutting, reining, working stock horse, hack and he did a great job in all of them. I gave a lot of reining and trail demonstrations on him without a bridle and he was a real popular horse in his time.'

Ian takes his physical strength for granted but it can come as a surprise to those who do not know him well. In his younger days he was deceptively wiry and Beryl recalls watching him rescue a foal that fell into a well by carrying it out on his shoulders. On another occasion they were on their way to a campdraft, towing Kings Gold in a hired float down a steep hill on the Peachester Range. The catch on the front door of the float worked its way open (it had been welded on upside down) and the hill was so steep that Goldy slid under the chest bar, partway out the door and ended up with his front hooves scraping along the bitumen. Ian just lifted him up – a grown horse – and put him back where he belonged. They continued on to the draft where Goldy won.

'WE COULD ALWAYS RELY ON HIM TOTALLY.'
JENNY KINGSTON, PAST EMPLOYER, CLIENT AND FRIEND

'HE'S A MASTER. IT REALLY IS UNFAIR THE ADVANTAGES HE'S GOT OVER US OTHER PEOPLE.'
JOHN STANTON, AUSTRALIAN LIVING RURAL LEGEND, MENTOR AND FRIEND

'NO ONE COMES NEAR HIM WHEN IT COMES TO YOUNG HORSES.'
LEXI PLATH, PAST STABLE MANAGER AND FRIEND

'DON'T USE TIME OR WORDS CARELESSLY, NEITHER CAN BE RETRIEVED.'

Ian had two major clients, Kolora Stud and John Elliot, who gave him a constant stream of breakers and show horses, all of which he broke and trained alone. In a freak accident in 1980 Ian tore the top off his thumb and while he was recovering he agreed to take on a young librarian who loathed her job and wanted to work with horses. Lexi Plath had messed with horses most of her life but at nineteen had never ridden a horse that was so well educated and as light in the mouth as the young horses she discovered at Ian's. As Ian was unable to ride because his thumb was stitched into his stomach, Lexi's first job in her three-week trial was to take over riding twelve young breakers and, in spite of her inexperience with green horses, she says, 'I never felt unsafe and I soon knew the job wasn't going to be boring.' Ian describes Lexi as a gutsy and fearless rider and her professionalism, attention to detail, love for the day-to-day care of the horses and ability to work as hard as him made the pair a formidable team. He said, 'Lexi's contribution was so much the foundation of my business. She is very methodical, has remarkable stamina and never seemed to be working hard.' Her three-week trial working for Ian lasted for eighteen years.

At the beginning of the 1980s La Terre Riante was deep in drought and the beef industry remained in a severe depression. Ian's popularity as a horse trainer had increased to the extent where horses were becoming more profitable than cattle so John Kingston, with Beryl's support, suggested Ian should become a full-time professional trainer. Ian admits to being very apprehensive. 'The idea frightened me to death because rarely had anyone done it successfully in a business sense before. I knew it would be a huge challenge and an uphill battle to make it profitable and I wondered if I would be up to the task.' He says, 'My great regret about this period is that it took me so long to understand that all I needed to do to change my life was to change my attitude - I am living proof that if you keep doing what you're doing you'll keep getting what you're getting.' He was so right in his prediction that it would be a tough battle but he was to prove more than equal to the challenge. Harrami was too remote to be viable as an accessible training centre so the partnership was dissolved, the property sold and Ian began looking for somewhere suitable to establish a horse training facility.

Jenny Kingston's King's Gaiety

Ian Showing Hug Me Doc, Nambour

'NO ONE IS MORE
HONEST THAN IAN.'

BARRY WHITAKER,
MENTOR AND FRIEND OF
MORE THAN 50 YEARS

'NO ONE GETS A
HORSE SOFTER AND
MORE BROKE. IAN CAN
MAKE A HOLLOW LOG
LOOK LIKE A BROKE
HOLLOW LOG.'

CLINTON ANDERSON,
USA CLINICIAN, PAST
EMPLOYEE AND FRIEND

CHAPTER 2 – IAN FRANCIS TRAINING STABLES

'ONLY THOSE WHO
RISK GOING TOO
FAR CAN POSSIBLY
FIND HOW FAR
THEY CAN GO.'

Ian's favourite working dog, 'Bear'

Filled with trepidation and self-doubt, in June 1981 Ian moved his family and Lexi to a bare 455 acre paddock at Widgee, west of Gympie in Queensland. Ian says, 'John Elliot suggested I look at Widgee where he had settled after selling Captain's Creek. I really liked the place but couldn't make the purchase price so John and Janette loaned me $40,000 to secure the deal. When I bought the property I subdivided some land and sold it to repay the loan - this was all done on a handshake deal and no contracts were exchanged. Later John and I went in different directions with our horses and I regret that I was not able to help them get where they wanted to go with their horse project.'

His concern that he was too old at thirty-six to set himself up as a professional horse trainer was compounded by a nagging fear that sceptical locals were right in saying he was crazy to establish his business in an area where they thought there were not enough horses to keep him in work. What would he do if his business failed? Was he wrong to believe he deserved to chase his dream? How would he support his family if no one sent horses to him?

Initially John Kingston and John Elliot sent him enough horses to make his new business a going concern but training horses was only part of the huge job that he faced. The only existing structures on the new property were a tiny, two-bedroom house, an old dairy and three broken-down yards. There was no fenc-

ing to speak of and no facilities for horses or cattle. Lexi remembers, 'We had horses coming out of our ears and nowhere to put them so we wired the sides of old cane bins together to make holding yards.' Jenny Kingston, as Ian's accountant, told him he needed to ride fifteen horses every day to pay his mortgage and feed his family so Ian planned to build eighteen stables, the additional three being for profit. The first eight stables were built by Inky McIntosh from timber cut by Barry Whitaker and John Elliot from their own properties and delivered to the local sawmill, and the remaining stables and infrastructure were built by Merv Christensen who spent years at Widgee, felling timber from the property for posts and cutting rails on the ground with his sleeper saw – a circular saw on wheels. The stress on Ian was enormous. He worked all hours of the day and night training horses, building yards and fences and

Outstanding, usable working facilities January 1985

Widgee Arena, complete with sand

worrying where the money would come from but slowly his dream began to take shape. The building work was gradual and on-going and as Ian earned a few more dollars Merv cut more timber and built another couple of stables or another yard.

Within a few years Ian's property sported indoor and outside stables, a floodlit arena, cattle yards, two round yards, stallion day yards, mare paddocks, a loading ramp and holding yard, a feed room, wash bay and hot walker. Ian also fenced the property to contain his herd of cattle. Jane Penfold joined the team, accepting Ian's offer of six weeks' employment to help prepare horses for the 1981 Rocky sale and staying for five and a half years. Jane says she first saw Ian in John Kingston's pharmacy in Maryborough and eavesdropped on his conversation with a photographer who wanted to film Ian starting a colt. Jane says she was impressed by what she heard, tracked Ian down and when they met discovered they had plenty in common. Jane had been at a loose end following the end of her marriage and the chance to work with horses came at a time when she was ready for change. Jane, Ian and Lexi prepared eighteen horses for that first sale team from Widgee and their horses more than doubled the sale average of $1227, achieving an average of $2600. Apart from preparation of sale horses, Jane describes her responsibilities as caretaker, offsider, mower of lawns and sounding board. She says, 'Ian liked someone to watch him work his horses and while I am not up to his standard I had been around horses all my life and could give him feedback about how the horses looked and how they were going. He always listened, but not just to me; he is always interested in what everyone has to say.'

Ian continued to worry about the lack of money, he felt he had the weight of the world on his shoulders and he sank into depression. He felt he had made an enormous mistake with this ambitious undertaking, he loathed being in debt and the bills kept piling up. Finding the money to put sand in the reining arena caused him many sleepless nights. He had reached an agreement with a local truckie that sand would be delivered when trucks were otherwise idle

The workers - Beryl, Jane and Lexi at Widgee in 1982

Three Fijians spent time with Ian at Widgee in February 1982 as part of an Australian Government Aid Program. In the round yard are Jane Penfold and Lexi Plath.

and Ian would pay the enormous bill of $2100 (the equivalent in today's terms of the cost of a new small car) when he could. He agonised over this debt until Jane reminded him he had not finalised his claim for Workers Compensation after losing the top off his thumb the previous year. A brief visit to the doctor was soon followed by a cheque for $2050 that paid for the sand and lightened his load.

While Ian, Lexi and Jane worked horses and Merv built the facilities for them, Beryl's time was fully taken up with collecting truckloads of hay and chaff, picking up rocks from the yards and paddocks, caring for the children and cooking for a constant stream of visitors. All visitors were impressed with the professionalism displayed by Ian and his team and particularly by Lexi who is a perfectionist. Stables and yards were always spotless and any horse could be taken straight from its stable into the show ring and win. Ian is adamant that Lexi's hard work and dedication to the preparation and presen-

'THERE'S NO ONE IN AUSTRALIA WHO HAS EQUALLED IAN'S RECORD IN COMPETITION. HE PUTS IN THE HOURS AND HE GETS THE RESULTS.'
JOHN KINGSTON, PAST EMPLOYER, CLIENT, MENTOR AND FRIEND

'YOU KNOW YOU ARE SAFE ON IAN'S HORSES. I WOULDN'T WANT TO RIDE A HORSE THAT HAD BEEN BROKEN IN BY ANYONE ELSE.'
LEXI PLATH, PAST STABLE MANAGER AND FRIEND

'HIS HORSES NEVER LOOK WORRIED; THEY ALWAYS KNOW WELL IN ADVANCE WHAT HE EXPECTS THEM TO DO.'
JANE PENFOLD, PAST EMPLOYEE AND FRIEND

'REMEMBER THIS
AND BE PURSUADED
OF ITS TRUTH.
SUCCESS IS NOT
IN THE HANDS OF
FATE, BUT WITHIN
OURSELVES.'

Jenny Kingston, Ian and King's Gaiety, Hi Point Snaffle Bit Horse at the 1982 Queensland QH Championships

King Ranch Caballero, 1982 Queensland State Champion Snaffle Bit Reining Horse

Beryl, Danny and Ian were joined by Lexi Plath and Jane Penfold when they celebrated their wedding anniversary in 1982 (Krissie was asleep under the table)

tation of show and sale horses played a major part in the success of his business.

Early in 1982 visitors to Widgee included three Fijians who arrived as part of a six million dollar Australian Government aid program to support an agricultural development project on Viti Levu, Fiji's largest island. The three came to Ian to gain experience in handling and breaking horses before returning to Fiji to manage the aid program. Ian continued his association with the five-year program when he went to Fiji for four weeks at the end of 1982 to break in a number of Fijian stock horses and to pass on his expertise to the men and boys who would be handling and using the horses. Ian's departure for Fiji came only days after a tough Rocky sale where he had presented fourteen horses for four clients and sold the highest and second-highest price mares for $4000 and $3500, and where his impressive sale average of $2567 was more than two-and-a-half-times the low sale average of $979. At the 1982 Queensland Quarter Horse Championships Ian received the Shamrock Stud Trophy for High Point Rider, the Lee Reborse Memorial Trophy, rode the High Point Snaffle Bit Horse, won the maiden hack with King's Gaiety and showed the State Champion Reining Horse, King Ranch Caballero. He also began holding regular horsemanship and horse-handling clinics throughout Queensland and NSW in 1982.

Lexi Plath explains that Ian's ability to jump from one thing to another without losing focus is a major reason for his success. She says, 'As soon as Ian finishes one event he focuses on the next and he never allows anything to distract him. As he drives away from the reining futurity he is focussed on the upcoming cutting futurity and as he drives home from that he focuses on the stock horse futurities.' Norma Whitley, a friend for more than forty years, concurs, saying, 'I have been at Widgee when Ian had several horses in training for the reining futurities, three or four for the stock horse futurities and another five or six for the cutting futurities. I can't describe how it is that he can get so much out of each and every one of them. He's a top athlete and he has heart and guts.' Ian's sister, Kay, says he was like that even as a kid, 'He has been able to totally focus his whole life.' Ken May, Ian's friend for more than thirty years, knows all about Ian's ability to focus. He says, 'One day Ian and I were riding young horses when a wild storm swept in. I got very nervous and started looking around which meant my horse got nervous too. Suddenly lightning struck a tree about three hundred metres away – it made a hell of a noise and there were bits of bark and splinters flying around. I said to Ian that maybe we should get out of the storm and he looked up and said, "What storm?" His horse was so focussed that it had not seen or heard the lightning strike either.'

There are many things that have contributed to Ian's success and one of the most important is his ability to learn from every person – horseman or not – with whom he comes in contact. John Kingston believes this is Ian's greatest gift. He says, 'He listens to everybody, internally digests it and decides what is relevant to him.' Ian is self-taught in almost everything he has done. He has had little formal riding instruction apart from a school in the early 1970s with Olympic dressage rider, Guy Creighton, and his wife, Ann. There he was confronted with

diagonals. He says, 'Diagonals were a total revelation to me. No one ever explained how important it is to take the correct diagonal and I struggled with them for years. I knew it was a correct tool and if you are a tradesman you use the correct tool so I persevered until I got it right.' Ian has successfully educated and ridden dressage horses and hacks, including Champion Station Hacks at Brisbane Royal, and he educated a brilliant thoroughbred that went on to be champion hack at Brisbane, Sydney and Melbourne Royal Shows when later owned by the Brisbane President of EFA Queensland. Ian explains, 'I believed that by exposing myself to different disciplines I would understand my clients' needs when they sent their good horses to me. I felt that I couldn't justify calling myself a trainer if I hadn't competed in every event that my clients compete in.' Ian has not only started hacks and dressage horses but also polocrosse horses, Arabians, Stock Horses, Paints, Quarter Horses, Appaloosas and Shetland ponies – but he only rode the Shetlands at dusk when no one could see him.

He soon became known as 'Mr Versatile', a description he considers to be the ultimate compli-

Ian and Hug Me Doc, 1992 NRHA Reining Futurity Reserve Champion, AQHA Championships Hi Point Junior Horse, Queensland QH Championships Hi Point Performance Horse 1991 & 1992

'I VALUE IAN AS SOMEONE WHO IS A FRIEND FOR LIFE, WHO WILL ALWAYS BE HONEST AND TELL ME THE TRUTH ABOUT MY HORSES AND WHO HAS MORE KNOWLEDGE IN HIS LITTLE FINGER THAN MOST OF US HAVE IN A LIFETIME.'
LEXIE BASTABLE, CLIENT AND FRIEND

'IT'S LIKE HE DANCES WITH HIS HORSES.'
JENNY BROWN, PAST EMPLOYEE AND FRIEND

'HE STRUGGLED HARD AT WIDGEE BUT HE DID IT.'
NORMA WHITLEY, FRIEND OF MORE THAN 40 YEARS

ment. His horses receive a complete education, no matter what their destiny is. Janet Twohill's dressage horse was unexpectedly lame at the Queensland Quarter Horse Championships. She ran into Ian who had just finished his final reining pattern aboard reining futurity winner Hug Me Doc and Ian immediately offered her the stallion to ride in place of her own good dressage horse. Janet said, 'We just swapped his saddle and Huggy and I went and won three out of four dressage tests – even though he was still wearing his sliders.' Hug Me Doc was bred by Jenny Kingston and he was one of a number of good Kolora horses that Ian put through Rocky Sale for her. He remembers, 'When we started him he was nice but he would hump around with the saddle on when he was fresh. One great memory I have is of Robyn Hanson, who came from a family of very capable riders and who worked for me in 1990, riding him in the round pen. Huggy was doing a fair job of humping up and she just threw the reins at him and laughed her head off. Robyn was later killed in a mustering accident, shortly before she was due to come back to work for me. I'll never understand such a terrible waste of such a young talent.'

Peter Bosanquet had bought Hug Me Doc at Rocky that year, paying the top sale price of $8000 before sending him back to Ian for further training. Ian showed Hug Me Doc to Reserve Champion at the NRHA Reining Futurity, high point junior horse at the AQHA Championships, high point junior horse and high point overall performance horse at the Queensland Quarter Horse Championships twice, he won other reining futurities and also won in trail, pleasure, hunter and western riding. Ian said, 'He was a great horse to have on the team and I put him in everything I could nominate him for.' In 1992 Peter Bosanquet decided to part with Huggy and Ian once again put him through Rocky sale, the stallion again setting a sale record when Lexie Bastable outbid Morning Sun Ranch for him. Ian said, 'I was really relieved when Lexie said she would retire Huggy to stud and not show him under saddle because she seemed too inexperienced to cope with a stud horse under show conditions.' Lexie says she will never forget the look on Ian's face after the sale, 'He

had to show me how to put Huggy's travelling boots on before I took him home – I told him I was inexperienced but I don't think he believed me until then!' Two weeks after the sale Ian received a call from Lexie. 'She was really excited and said, "I've ridden him and he's lovely" and I thought "bloody hell!" Another two weeks went by and she rang me again and said, "He is so lovely I'm going to show him" and that scared the hell out of me.' Ian continues, 'Well, Huggy looked after her and they have gone on to be one of the great success stories of the horse world. If everyone could get as much enjoyment from their horses as Lexie has with Hug Me Doc it would be great for them and great for the horse, they really prove that the outside of a horse is good for the inside of a man.'

In 1983 Reg Brown, a grazier from Nonda Downs near Julia Creek in far north Queensland, loaded two of his working stock horse mares on a train and sent them a distance of 2250km just so they could be educated and shown by Ian. Those sceptical local stockmen were still around and once again they shook their heads until Ian and Nonda Native Whimsey won Champion Station Hack against the best competition in the State at Brisbane Royal Show to a standing ovation from the 15,000-strong crowd. The five-year-old mare quaintly called The Turtle was claimed to have been the first Gulf Country horse ever to win a major title at a Brisbane Royal Show, a massive achievement for a mare who had previously been a mustering horse. Whimsey had really only travelled from Nonda Downs as a

Nonda Native Whimsey

companion to the $5000 filly, Jeannie Gunn, but when injury forced Jeannie Gunn's retirement Ian turned his attention to the travelling companion. Reg Brown's daughter, Heather, says she first saw Ian at the 1981 Rocky sale and thought to herself, 'There goes a horseman.' Heather was raised on the family cattle station, her grandfather had bred one Melbourne Cup winner and bought and raced a second and in her family true horsemanship was revered. She says, 'I was exposed to many good horsemen and I had spent a lifetime studying them and their relationships with horses so I felt I was in a unique position to judge Ian's ability.' Heather entrusted many more horses to Ian's care and has maintained a solid friendship with him to this day. Ian returned to Brisbane Royal to win the station hack class three times, working stock horse mare class twice as well as supreme working stock horse and numerous Quarter Horse classes including Champion Stallion with Jenny Kingston's Kings Charge in 1983 who also won the bridle path hack and western pleasure classes that year. 1983 was also the year that Ian began winning reining futurities when Gold Astral and Honey Belle took out champion and reserve in the reining futurity at Nambour.

Ian worked long hours breaking and educating horses of every persuasion for any discipline while developing his property and showing horses for his clients. The awards and accolades flowed, with wins in 1984 in reined cow horse, trail, western pleasure and reining futurities and maturities, the high point snaffle bit horse

Kings Charge

at the AQHA Championships, State Champion titles in reining, cow horse and trail and high point rider and high point junior horse at the Queensland Quarter Horse Championships. Ian was everywhere, always mounted on impeccably presented, relaxed horses and always ready with a smile, a word of encouragement or just a 'gidday', whether he knew you or not.

He says he knew a man who had lost an arm in an accident and who needed a good horse to use on his cattle property. He mentioned to this man that he had a horse that was born to do that job, 'He laughed and said he had heard that story before but he saw Kings Gold work one day and changed his attitude. This man became about my best friend until he convinced me that he needed Goldy more than I did but once I let him have him he didn't seem to need to be my best friend any more. I gained a little experience out of that.' Goldy's sale price of $2650 was an Australian record for a Stock Horse. Ian had hoped to replace Kings Gold with another horse for himself but he realised if he continued to ride horses of his own he lost income so he began breeding horses to sell on the condition that the good ones returned to him to be trained.

The wins continued as horses of every size, shape, disposition and ability arrived at Widgee for a touch of the Ian Francis magic. In 1985 Dan's Lady Cylip was the AQHA high point working cow horse of the year, high point working cow horse for Queensland, State cow horse champion, Australian Reined Cow Horse

Gold Astral

'IAN FRANCIS CHANGED MY LIFE.'
LEXIE BASTABLE, CLIENT AND FRIEND

'IAN FRANCIS HAS A TREMENDOUS CONNECTION WITH A HORSE. IT COMES FROM THE CORE OF HIS BEING.'
HEATHER PASCOE (NEE BROWN), CLIENT AND FRIEND

'IT DIDN'T REALLY MATTER WHICH HORSE HE GOT ON, HE TURNED EVERY ONE INTO A CHAMPION IN ITS OWN RIGHT.'
FRANK GREEN, TRAINER, PAST EMPLOYEE AND FRIEND

Ian and Murrumbo Fiona

Photo: Kenyon Sports
Photography

*Vestal Morn, 1989 Garden City Stakes Western Pleasure
Futurity Champion, SQQHA Trail Futurity Champion*

Association cow horse futurity reserve champion and Moonbi and SQQHA reining futurity champion while Heather Brown's Yarranoo Reggae was Moonbi cow horse futurity reserve champion and Star Carousel won reining futurities. D.Bar Paint Your Wagon ran reserve reining futurity champion to Star Carousel, and just to keep the onlookers interested, Ardo Docs Pretender won the SQQHA halter futurity.

In 1985 Ian and Beryl parted. Beryl and the children left the property, eventually settling in the country town of Nambour where Beryl had a successful career in real estate, market research and security and now works for the late Steve Irwin's Australia Zoo. She knew Steve personally long before he became famous and says, 'He was a lovely guy and what you saw was exactly what you got.'

In 1986 Ian won his first Widgee Stock Horse Futurity with Cathy Marsh's three-year-old Whisp O'Lena and over the next five years he twice won and once placed second in the Widgee two-year-old futurity with Nonda Tall Poppy, Nonda Music Man and Havenville Sally Ann, won the Widgee three-year-old futurity three times more with Vogue O'Lena, Havenville Crackshot and Donrica Conchita and placed second with Dead Eye Doc and also won the Widgee four-year-old futurity with Havenville Gentle Abby. The delightful Murrumbo Fiona hit the show scene in 1986 by winning two reining futurities and D.Bar Paint Your Wagon (Wags) won enough cow horse futurities to be the AQHA high point cow horse of the year, giving Ian his second consecutive award in this event. At the Queensland Quarter Horse Championships Ian was high point rider and piloted Wags to a Queensland State Champion working cow horse title; he won trail and western pleasure futurities on Kolora Dynasty, another western pleasure futurity on Kolora Classic and his own weanling colt, Hoodoo Voodoo, won five halter futurities. At the annual Moonbi Futurity Show, Ian and Star Carousel won the cow horse futurity and Ian also placed third in this event with D.Bar Paint Your Wagon and fourth with Whisp O'Lena. At Moonbi the following year Ian was high point rider, Hoodoo Voodoo continued his winning way by beating the country's best yearlings in the yearling halter futurity and Murrumbo Fiona won the reining futurity with Tweed Doc N Wood close on her heels as reserve champion. Ian attended all the big shows in 1987; he won his first Cloncurry Stockman's Challenge with Star Carousel who was also the highest-scoring Australian Stock Horse, won the prestigious Queensland Reined Cow Horse Futurity with Murrumbo Fiona and placed third with Tweed Doc N Wood. At the same show he won the reining futurity with Kaylen Silver Threads and Kolora Double Bar was the hackamore cow horse champion, high point hackamore cow horse and high point hackamore reining horse.

John Stanton commented, 'A lot of people, the horse they ride this year will be the same as the horse they rode last year and the year before that, they put their horses in a mould. Ian has the ability to take his horses further; he polishes them and shows people a better horse each time.' At the 1987 AQHA Championships Ian showed the AQHA National Champion trail horse, Kolora Classic and the National Champion snaffle bit reining horse and National Champion cow horse, Murrumbo Fiona, with Tweed Doc N Wood placing fourth and Kolora Double Bar fifth in both these events. Ian took out nine state titles at the Queensland and NSW Quarter Horse Championships, won reining futurities with Murrumbo Fiona and Kaylen Silver Threads, a bridle path hack futurity with Kolora Lunar Lady, a western pleasure futurity with Kolora Classic and halter futurities with Hoodoo Voodoo and Elite O Lena. Murrumbo Fiona was the AQHA high point reining horse of the year and AQHA high point working cow horse of the year for 1987 and received the Greg Lougher Memorial Trophy for reining horse of the year. During this busy year Ian also managed to find time to run a number of schools and clinics throughout Queensland and NSW.

In 1988 Ian was inducted into the AQHA Hall of Fame for setting standards of excellence across a broad spectrum in the Australian Quarter Horse industry by his extraordinary personal example, his generosity of spirit and his professionalism in and out of the show ring. Ian is highly regarded in the Quarter Horse world not only for his ability as a trainer but also for his honesty and integrity and his willingness to help anyone at any time, whether they are his students, clients or competitors. He is renowned for helping others who have problems with their horses and will help right up until the moment these people enter the show ring and attempt to beat him. He is generous with his time, knowledge and advice and he credits the late Lee Reborse with shaping his attitude about sharing information. 'Until I met Lee, anyone I asked how they did what they did would say, "It took me thirty years to learn so you spend thirty years learning it too." I soon realised that perhaps these people didn't know or weren't articulate enough to explain what they were do-

ing so they covered it by not sharing. Lee had a very open attitude towards sharing information and believed it was a good thing if he explained something to you and you came back and beat him.' Ian's admiration for his mentor led him to adopt the same attitude but he takes it one step further; all he asks when he helps someone is that they, in turn, help someone else as he believes if you do good it will be returned many times. He recalls arriving late at the Tamworth Showgrounds for the AQHA Championships one year. He unloaded his horses and was looking for a place to park his truck when Janet Gill told him that Bernard McAneney was stranded with four horses 140 km away. Ian immediately drove the distance to pick them up because he could. Fifteen years later, on his way to Victoria towing a new trailer with a big load of horses, his tyres blew, one after another. He was in the middle of nowhere, out of spare tyres when who should stop and offer him a ride to the nearest town but Janet Gill. Ian feels this was more than coincidence.

Cheryl Anderson recalls that when her son, Clinton, who previously spent twelve months working for Ian, first competed in reining he sent his mare, Pillamindi Doll, to Ian for six weeks before the reining futurities. Ian trained Mindy, knowing Clinton would do his utmost to beat him on the day, and he offered support and encouragement right up until the moment Clinton rode into the arena. Cheryl said, 'It meant so much to us that Ian helped our son, we saw it as a true sign of his sportsmanship.' Clinton placed behind Ian in the reining futurity by half a point. Soon after the futurity, Clinton departed for America where he is now one of the most successful clinicians that country has known. He tapped into a section of the market that is ignored by other clinicians, baby boomers and trail riders, and in 2006 alone he grossed US $10 million. Every year Clinton invites Ian to the US to conduct clinics with him and at his clinics and workshops he constantly thanks his Aussie mentor and says, 'Seventy percent of what I teach I learned from Ian Francis'.

Ian continued his winning way in the late 1980s and throughout the 1990s at the reining futurities, cow horse futurities, stock horse futurities,

'HE NEVER LIES TO YOU ABOUT YOUR HORSE AND HE WILL NEVER DO THE WRONG THING BY YOU.'
LEXIE BASTABLE, CLIENT AND FRIEND

'IAN FRANCIS IS THE BEST HORSEMAN IN THE WORLD.'
CLINTON ANDERSON, US CLINICIAN, PAST EMPLOYEE AND FRIEND

'HE'S THE BEST HORSEMAN I KNOW.'
JOHN STANTON, AUSTRALIAN LIVING LEGEND, MENTOR AND FRIEND

'YOU CANNOT LOSE IF YOU DON'T QUIT, OR YOU DON'T START.'

Ian describes Sassy Lassie as one of the best futurity horses he'd ever bred and started. Frank Green bought her and prepared her for the stockman's challenges and cutting futurities.

The NZ Youth Team with their Aussie trainer: Marilyn Lemburg (manager), Karla Jamieson, Gayle Falconer (assistant manager), Jozette Thode, Ian riding Rusty Frame's bull, Claire Donaldson, Carol Anderson and Fleur Falconer.

halter futurities, trail futurities, hunter under saddle futurities and at the AQHA Championships, Queensland and NSW Quarter Horse Championships, and he was a regular in the AQHA end of year awards. In August 1989 Pat Parelli conducted a special clinic at Ian Francis Training Stables as part of his Australian tour and in August 1990 Ian travelled to the USA following a testimonial dinner hosted by Brian and Mary Green, held in his honour on the eve of the Widgee Stock Horse Futurities. Ian's friends, colleagues and admirers donated $6000 to send him to the States where he spent time with reining trainers, Tim McQuay and Bob Loomis. At his testimonial dinner, friend and client, Susie Penfold described Ian as, 'Much more than a good horseman; he is a great winner, a good loser, a top yarn-spinner, a tolerant and constant friend and a great Australian.' Susie continued, 'This cheque is not a payment. We can never repay him for turning our horses into champions, for the pure joy of watching him produce a per-

fect reining run, for his many contributions to the horse world, for his friendship. It is not even a gift. It is a testimony to the admiration, respect and affection in which we hold him.'

In 1991, the same year that he won the Monto two-year-old, three-year-old and four-year-old stock horse futurities, Ian cracked his first win in the coveted NCHA cutting futurity with the filly, Spindle, repeating this NCHA futurity win in 2003 with One Hellofa Spin and again in 2005 with Gidgee Coals. He and One Hellofa Spin returned to Tamworth in 2004 to win the NCHA Derby. This really is a considerable effort considering Ian also won reining, stock horse and western performance futurities and prepared and presented horses at Rocky sale during many of the years he trained cutters. How many other professional cutting trainers can do that? In 1992 Ian won his first NRHA Futurity Champion title riding Amaroos Rock N Return owned by Morning Sun Ranch, and in another first was Futurity Reserve Champion on Hug Me Doc owned by Peter Bosanquet. This was the first of five NRHA Futurity wins over the next ten years, during which time he also trained and rode four NRHA futurity reserve champions, four NRHA derby champions and four NRHA derby reserve champions.

Also in 1992 Ian managed the New Zealand youth team at the Youth World Cup in Tamworth and was a member of the Australian team that placed second at the International Reining World Cup in Canada. To represent your country in international competition is considered to be the pinnacle of sporting achievement and to win against the world's best is an unattainable dream for most, but not for Ian. He returned to Canada the following year and after only two rides on his allocated horse, was IRC Open Division World Reining Champion. In 1994 Ian received a medal for outstanding achievement in sport at the Kilkivan Shire Australia Day Awards, receiving the Shire's senior sports award at the 2003 Australia Day Awards. He again won the Cloncurry Stockman's Challenge with Docs Gold Dude in 1996, has given reining and cutting demonstrations twice at Equitana Asia-Pacific and at Horse Australia and Beef Australia, he was Equitana Masters Reining

Champion in 2001, in 2006 was named an NRHA Rider Legend and Mitavite Living Legend and in 2007 Ian was inducted into the NCHA Hall of Fame after having won more than $500,000 in cutting competition.

Lexi and Ian parted company in 1998 and, after working for Robert Woodward of Garrison Stud in Victoria where she cared for Doc's Spinifex in his last months, and holidaying with Stephen and Sue King and their children in the USA, Lexi now works for her brother, managing his tyre business in Brisbane.

Late in 2003 Ian fulfilled his childhood dream of owning a cattle property when he bought 700 acres at Murgon, west of Gympie in Queensland. He named the new property Took-a-While and says, 'Yes, it took a long time to realise this dream but I didn't want to buy anything until I could afford to pay cash for it. We moved here in January 2004 and I can now more diligently pursue my cutting ambitions because I can access more fresh cattle for training my horses.' Ian had a lot of 'help' preparing for the move. 'Every time I turned my back or went away, Virginia Lemon, Paul Banham and Les Powell took truckloads of stuff to the tip. They decided that anything that hadn't been used for a while had to go and what was left they put in a garage sale. I won't say I ran around the district buying things back but boy, I could use some of that stuff now.'

When you walk into Ian's home you are surrounded by reminders of his phenomenal success. The walls in his lounge and dining room are covered with photos, and trophies and buckles cover every available surface. Displayed prominently amongst these treasured memories is a photo of a young man with a prosthetic leg, running a marathon. Canadian, Terry Fox, was an active teenager who was diagnosed with bone cancer after complaining of knee pain. He was only eighteen when he was forced to have his right leg amputated fifteen centimetres above the knee and while he was in hospital he was so overcome by the suffering of other cancer patients, many of them only young children, that he decided to run across Canada to raise money for cancer research. He called his journey the Marathon of Hope. Terry covered five thousand

Docs Gold Dude, 1995 AQHA National Champion Junior Reining Horse, 1996 AQHA National Champion Cow Horse, AQHA National Champion Western Riding Horse, Hi Point Junior Horse

When the pain from old injuries becomes overwhelming Ian gains inspiration from young Canadian cancer victim, Terry Fox, and finds the strength to get out of bed and face another day

'PEOPLE TRY TO UNDERMINE YOU AND IAN DOES THE OPPOSITE. HE IS NOT HUNG UP ABOUT SHARING HIS KNOWLEDGE.'
VIVIAN WEARING, INSTRUCTOR, MENTOR AND FRIEND

'HIS HORSES LEARN THE JOB, THEY LEARN QUICKLY AND THEY RETAIN IT FOREVER.'
SUE FRANKS, INSTRUCTOR AND CLIENT

'DON'T LET ANYBODY'S OPINION KILL YOUR BELIEF IN YOURSELF.'

N Bar Dot King Poco Bar 1990

kilometres in eighteen months as he conditioned his body before he began the Marathon of Hope by dipping his leg in the Atlantic Ocean at St John's on 12 April 1980. He ran for 143 days and 5373 kilometres, covering forty-two kilometres each day before the cancer spread to his lungs and he was forced to abandon the run. He died on 28 June 1981, a month before his twenty-third birthday. To date, more than four hundred million dollars has been raised worldwide for cancer research through the annual Terry Fox Run, held across Canada and the world. When the pain of the many injuries Ian has suffered throughout his career becomes too much, he looks at that photo of Terry Fox and is thankful to still have his life and two functioning legs, even if they do not function very well.

Ian is sixty-two this year and faces major surgery to reconstruct his left knee which has seemed like a target for injury since he was sixteen. It has taken direct hits from horses and cattle; it has been rolled on, fallen on, kicked and fallen on again. He underwent a shoulder reconstruction ten years ago and broke his right leg in 2002 when a mare somersaulted over on top of him. One of the most life-threatening injuries he has suffered was in 2000 when a mare flipped over

backwards as soon as he mounted, leaving him lying in the sand with torn hips and a ruptured stomach lining. However, in typical fashion he says the injuries that pain him the most are those he gives himself when he beats his head against brick walls, trying to get his message through to non-pros and clinic attendees.

Ian has no plans to slow down or retire; instead he says he will refocus his energies in other directions once he knows the outcome of his knee surgery. He says, 'I have changed direction in my career many times – when I moved from campdrafting to cow horse, then to western performance, then to reining, then to cutting and now I am looking forward to conducting more clinics. The bend in the road is not the end of the road unless you fail to take the turn and I see this as an opportunity to take on more challenges.' He would like to continue training but is realistic enough to accept that another change may be forced on him. He says he has fulfilled all the things he wanted to do for other people, winning futurities and making their horses shine in public, but he maintains the high point of his life and his career is still to come. Over the past thirty years, Ian has campaigned a steady stream of exceptional horses from untried weanlings to national champions and national futurity winners in every sphere of western performance but he has educated many more horses that went on to win under the guidance of their owners and other professional trainers. He judged rodeo for twelve years, has been an AQHA and HSAA judge for over twenty years, has judged all over Australia, New Zealand and in New Caledonia and has ridden and won in every class he has ever judged.

Ian always thought that because he has exceptional feel, timing and balance and the ability to get a horse to understand him, that everyone could do it. It took him many years to recognise that what he has is a gift that is not bestowed upon many other riders. There will never be another Ian Francis, a horseman who lives, breathes, eats, sleeps and thinks horses and cattle, who spent his formative years learning his craft and a lifetime honing it and has given back to his industry far more than he has ever received.

Kolora Classic

Photo: Kenyon Sports Photography

Kolora Lunar Lady

Photo: Kenyon Sports Photography

Kolora Double Bar

'I HAVE NEVER SEEN A HORSE ACT AGGRESSIVELY TOWARDS IAN.'

LEXI PLATH, PAST STABLE MANAGER AND FRIEND

'DON'T EVER BE FOOLED INTO THINKING THIS HAS BEEN A GLAMOROUS, EASY ROAD OR HAS COME WITHOUT A HELL OF A COST IN WEAR AND TEAR ON MIND AND BODY. I SOMETIMES WONDER IF OUR YOUNG STARS TODAY HAVE A CLUE HOW HARD IT REALLY WAS IN THE 1970S. IAN FRANCIS HAD TO BE AN INVENTOR, A PIONEER, A TRAIL-BLAZER FOR THE REST OF US.'

TED HINTZ, SHOW, RODEO AND CUTTING COMMENTATOR OF 40 YEARS AND FRIEND

'THERE ARE MANY GOOD HORSEMEN BUT IAN IS A COMPLETE HORSEMAN.'

FRANK GREEN, TRAINER, PAST EMPLOYEE AND FRIEND

'ALL THE THINGS I KNOW AT THE TOP, I LEARNED AT THE BOTTOM.'

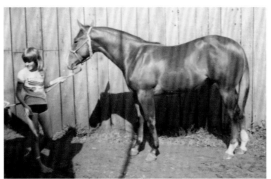

Kris Ann with the yearling Hoodoo Voodoo

'I bred a colt called Hoodoo Voodoo and won a bunch of halter futurities and maturities with him. We were pretty high on the colt but lost him when he was a two-year-old. About a week later his mother, Doc's Lyric, had a real fancy-looking colt by Beaver Doc so I called him The Equalizer. He soon got to thinking that he was the best looking horse around and I don't believe anyone was able to convince him otherwise. He had the prettiest head I have seen on a colt and had great presence in the show ring with an attitude like, "We all know who the winner is so let's get the champion ribbon on and get the hell out of here." I sold him to Frank Lee from Roma in Queensland and showed him for Frank for a while. I bought him back and gelded him when he proved to be infertile and he's probably the only horse to win the AQHA Championships as a colt and later as a gelding. Under saddle Mac had a real slow lope and was a natural lead changer and was great in pleasure, trail and western riding.

I also showed him in hunter, reining and working cow horse but they were not his

Photo: Kenyon Sports Photography

The Equalizer at six months

34

Photo: Karalinga

Retread (Half brother to Hoodoo Voodoo and The Equalizer), bred by Ian

real strengths. Because I owned him and had other commitments to clients' horses Lexi showed him – although I don't know why she liked him so much because he was a cheeky little buggar and gave her a hard time. He would mess her around so I'd take him and he'd just lope along like butter wouldn't melt in his mouth – it used to make her madder than hell! John Farnham was looking for a horse to learn cow horse on and Jill rang one day and asked about Mac. I thought he would do the job so she bought him sight unseen but poor John never got a look-in. When Mac came off the transport truck and Jill saw him I don't know if John got to even pat him. Jill's partnership with Mac has

been well-documented and they have a great record of achievement and I, as his breeder, have had a lot of enjoyment from seeing him do such a good job for her.'
Ian Francis

Photo: Karalinga

Wouldnt It Roc Ya (Half Brother to Hoodoo Voodoo, The Equalizer and Retread), bred by Ian

'HE WOULD TELL ME DIRTY JOKES SO I WOULD RELAX BEFORE A SHOWMANSHIP CLASS.'
MARIE ALBURY, CLIENT

'HE DOESN'T TAKE THE HORSE OUT OF THE HORSE AND HE DOESN'T GET IN THE WAY OF THE HORSE.'
JOHN STANTON, AUSTRALIAN LIVING LEGEND, MENTOR AND FRIEND

Photo: Julie Wilson

Ian was inducted into the AQHA Hall of Fame in 1988. He is shown here with AQHA Director, Ricky Glen

On being in credit with Ian…
'*Somewhere in the mid 1980s I was on my way to Scone with six horses for the NSW Quarter Horse Championships. Three hours down the road, at Warwick, I burned out the clutch and there was some doubt that parts would get there in time to allow me to make it to the show. I knew a couple of people who had trailers big enough to haul six horses and I felt I may have had enough credit with them to ask for help, so I rang and asked if either of them had any ideas on what I could do. Now, these were two successful businessmen but all of a sudden they were brain-dead and couldn't*

figure out what they could do. I knew John Osborne lived near Warwick but I barely knew him other than to say hello to and he sure didn't owe me any favours. I found his number, called and asked if there were any local options in case my truck wasn't repaired in time. John said, "That's easy. You just come and get my truck and go." Then he offered to come and pick me up. This is why I like to live in the country and am proud to be part of cowboy culture. My truck was fixed in time and I did not need John's help but John Osborne and his family have lots of credit at my place anytime.' Ian Francis

AQHA CHAMPIONSHIPS, NATIONAL CHAMPIONS AND HIGH POINT WINS

1984
Hi Point Snaffle Bit Horse .... Kings Charge
National Champion Halter Stallion .... Kings Charge

1987
National Champion Trail Horse .... Kolora Classic
National Champion Snaffle Bit Reining Horse ... Murrumbo Fiona
National Champ. Snaffle Bit Working Cow Horse .... Murrumbo Fiona

1988
National Champion Halter Horse .... Hi in the Sky
National Champion Junior Reining Horse Murrumbo Fiona
National Champion Junior Cow Horse .... Murrumbo Fiona
National Champion SB Working Cow Horse Vogue O'Lena
National Champ. SB Western Riding Horse N Bar Dot King Poco Bar

1989
National Champion SB Working Cow Horse .. B.S. Mingo's Lucero
National Champion 3YO colt .... Rock the Deck
Hi Point Snaffle Bit/Hackamore Horse .... Rock the Deck
Hi Point Junior Horse

1990
National Champion Gelding .... N Bar Dot King Poco Bar
National Champion Junior Trail .. N Bar Dot King Poco Bar
National Champion Snaffle Bit Trail Horse .... The Equalizer
National Champion Western Riding Horse
National Champion Working Cow Horse
Reserve National Champion Gelding .... The Equalizer
Hi Point Junior Horse .... The Equalizer
Hi Point Snaffle Bit Horse .... Nonda Tall Poppy

1991
Reserve National Champ. SB/H Reining Horse .... Nonda Humphrey Oak
National Champion SB/H Working Cow Horse .... The Equalizer
Hi Point Junior Horse

1992
National Champion Junior Cutting Horse .... Spindle
National Champion SB/H Reining Horse .... Hug Me Doc
National Champion Halter Gelding .... The Equalizer
National Champion SB/H Working Cow Horse .... The Equalizer
Hi Point Junior Horse .... The Equalizer
R/U Hi Point Junior Horse .... Hug Me Doc

1993
National Champion 4YO Reining Derby .. Amaroos Rock N Return
National Champion Junior Reining .... Amaroos Rock N Return
National Champion Junior Trail .... Docs Kylie Ann
National Champion Junior Western Riding Docs Kylie Ann

1994
Reserve National Champ. Senior Reining Amaroos Rock N Return
Reserve National Champion Junior Trail ..... Pillamindi Roc

1995
National Champion Open Working Cow Horse .... Doc Paperweight
National Champion Senior Reining Horse .... Authentic Roc
National Champion Junior Reining Horse Docs Gold Dude
Hi Point Senior Horse .... Authentic Roc
R/U Hi Point Junior Horse .... Doc's Gold Dude

1996
National Champion Junior Western Riding Horse ...... Docs Gold Dude
National Champion Open Cow Horse ...... Docs Gold Dude
National Champion 2YO Trail Horse ...... Pretty Moving Mr
Reserve National Champion Junior Trail Horse .. Docs Gold Dude
Reserve National Champ. Junior Reining Horse Docs Gold Dude
Reserve National Champ. Senior Reining Horse .... Hug Me Doc
Reserve National Champion Senior Trail Horse .. Authentic Roc
Hi Point Junior Horse .... Docs Gold Dude

1997
National Champion Junior Reining Horse .... Riverholme Royal Oak

1999
National Champion Junior Reining Horse Sachem Lillipilli

MAJOR WESTERN PERFORMANCE, FUTURITY AND HIGH POINT WINS

1981
QQHA Championships Supreme Halter Horse .. Angelique
QQHA State Champion Halter Gelding under 6 yrs ... Pines Gold Bar

1982
QQHA Shamrock Stud Hi Point Rider –
Lee Reborse Memorial Trophy .... Ian Francis
QQHA Championships Hi Point Snaffle Bit Horse .... Kings Gaiety
QQHA State Champion Maiden Hack .... Kings Gaiety
QQHA State Champion SB Reining Horse .... King Ranch Caballero

1983
SQQHA Bridle Path Hack Futurity .... Kings Charge
SEQPHA Series Hi Point Snaffle Bit Horse .... Kings Charge
Brisbane Royal Champion Stallion .... Kings Charge

1984
QQHA Shamrock Stud Hi Point Rider .... Ian Francis
QQHA State Champion Reining Horse .... Gold Astral
QQHA State Champion Working Cow Horse .. Honey Belle
QQHA Hi Point Snaffle Bit Horse .... Kings Charge
SEQPHC Trail Futurity Champion .... Kings Charge

> 'HE'S A WONDERFUL HUMAN BEING. HE HAS IMPECCABLE MANNERS AND IS A LOYAL AND TRUSTWORTHY FRIEND.'
> JANET TWOHILL, CLIENT AND FRIEND OF MORE THAN FORTY YEARS

> 'HE WAS MY INSPIRATION, ALWAYS THERE WHEN I HIT A BAD SPOT AND WITHOUT HIM I NEVER WOULD HAVE ACHIEVED WHAT I DID.'
> MARIE ALBURY, CLIENT

'GOOD CHARACTER IS HARDER TO DEVELOP THAN TALENT. TALENT IS, TO SOME EXTENT A GIFT. CHARACTER HOWEVER IS DEVELOPED BY THOUGHT, CHOICE, COURAGE AND DETERMINATION.'

Docs Kylie Ann, CQQHA Futurity Show, Twilight Stakes Versatility Champion

SEQPHC Western Pleasure Futurity Champ . Kings Charge
SEQPHA Hi Point Snaffle Bit Horse................ Kings Charge
SQQHA Bridle Path Hack Futurity Champion .... Kings Charge
SQQHA Halter Futurity .... Kolora Classic

1985
SQQHA Halter Futurity Champion ... Ardo Docs Pretender
QQHA State Champion Working Cow Horse ... Dan's Lady Cylip
QQHA Hi Point Working Cow Horse Queensland .... Dan's Lady Cylip

1986
Nambour Western Pleasure Futurity Champion....... Kolora Classic
QQHA State Champ. Working Cow HorseD.Bar Paint Your Wagon
QQHA Championships Hi Point Rider .... Ian Francis
QQHA State Champion Senior Reining Horse........ Karinya Chadwick
SEQPHC Trail Futurity Champion.............. Kolora Dynasty
SEQPHC Western Pleasure Futurity Champion .... Kolora Dynasty
SEQQHA Yearling Colt Futurity Champion............ Hoodoo Voodoo
SEQQHA Hi Point Halter Horse................. Hoodoo Voodoo
SQQHA Weanling/Yearling Colt Futurity Champ.Hoodoo Voodoo
T&DQHA Supastock Colt Futurity Champion........ Hoodoo Voodoo
T&DQHA Supreme QH Exhibit.................. Hoodoo Voodoo

1987
T&DQHA Pleasure Challenge Champion
CQQHA Hi Point Hackamore Horse ..... Kolora Double Bar
CQQHA Hi Point Western Performance Horse......... Kolora Double Bar
CQQHA Hi Point Stallion....................... Kolora Double Bar
Moonbi Yearling Halter Futurity Champion .... Hoodoo Voodoo
Moonbi Futurities Hi Point Rider........................ Ian Francis
SEQQHA Western Pleasure Futurity Champion....... Kolora Classic

SEQQHA BP Hack Futurity Champion Kolora Lunar Lady
QQHA Champs BP Hack Futurity Champion........... Kolora Classic
QQHA Championships Hi Point Junior Horse .... Kolora Double Bar
QQHA Champs. Hi Point Performance Horse.......... Kolora Double Bar
QQHA State Champion SB Reining Horse..........Murrumbo Fiona
QQHA State Champion Western Riding Horse......... Kolora Double Bar
QQHA State Champion Working Cow Horse ....Murrumbo Fiona
QQHA Championships Hi Point Snaffle Bit Horse .. Kolora Classic
SQQHA Weanling Filly Futurity... Lazy D Leo's Somemore
SQQHA Yearling Filly Futurity Champion...... Elite O Lena
SQQHA Yearling Colt Futurity ChampionHoodoo Voodoo
Premier State Champion Working Cow Horse...Murrumbo Fiona
Premier State Champion Reining Horse...Murrumbo Fiona
Premier State Show Hi Point Snaffle Bit Horse ..Murrumbo Fiona

1988
AQHA Hi Point Halter Horse of the Year .... Lazy D Leo's Somemore
QQHA State Champion Snaffle Bit Cow Horse.......... Vogue O'Lena
QQHA State Champion Junior Cow Horse.........Murrumbo Fiona
QQHA State Champion Western Riding Horse..Murrumbo Fiona
QQHA Championships Hi Point Snaffle Bit Horse ... Vogue O'Lena G&WWPC Western Pleasure Spectacular .... Riverholme Royal Chex
Garden City Stakes Weanling Futurity Champion ....The Equalizer
NEQHA Pre-Nationals HUS Futurity ChampionTime for a Scotch
NEQHA Pre-Nationals Pleasure Futurity Champ. Time for a Scotch
NSWQHA Hi Point Snaffle Bit Horse .... Vogue O'Lena
Premier State Champion Junior Cow Horse ....Murrumbo Fiona
Premier State Champion Snaffle Bit Reining Horse... Vogue O'Lena
Premier State Champion Snaffle Bit Cow Horse .... Vogue O'Lena
Premier State Champion Western Riding Horse .... Vogue O'Lena
Premier State Show Hi Point Snaffle Bit Horse .... Vogue O'Lena
SEQQHA Halter Futurity Champion..............The Equalizer
SEQQHA Yearling Futurity Champion ....The Equalizer
SEQQHA BP Hack Futurity Champion Kolora Lunar Lady
SQQHA Weanling Futurity Champion...........The Equalizer
SQQHA Futurity/Maturity Colt Champion..The Equalizer
SQQHA Supreme Futurity/Maturity Champion...........The

Equalizer
SQQHA Bicentennial Trail Futurity Champion......... Kolora
Lunar Lady
SQQHA Bicentennial Halter Maturity Champion .Rock the
Deck
SQQHA Spectacular Versatility Trail Champ .... Nareeb
Nareeb Pirouette
SQQHA Spectacular Versatility HUS Champ........... Nareeb
Nareeb Pirouette
SQQHA Spectacular Versatility Pleasure Champ .... Nareeb
Nareeb Pirouette

1989
Garden City Stakes Western Pleasure Futurity Ch .....Vestal
Morn Nambour Halter Maturity Champion.......... Easy Doc
QQHA Championships Hi Point Rider .... Ian Francis
QQHA Championships Halter Futurity Champion ....The
Equalizer
QQHA Championships BP Hack Futurity Champ .....Vestal
Morn
QQHA State Champion Reining HorseB.S. Mingo's Lucero
QRCHA All Breeds Halter Futurity Champion...............The
Equalizer
QRCHA Halter Maturity Champion... Widecombes Classic
Gold
SQQHA Futurities BP Hack Futurity Champion ...Rock the
Deck
SQQHA Futurities Halter Futurity Champ.................Shines

Magnolia Bid
SQQHA Futurities Trail Futurity Champion ....Vestal Morn
T&DQHA Futurities Pleasure Futurity Champ......Rock the
Deck
T&DQHA Futurities Halter Futurity Champion.............The
Equalizer

1990
Dubbo Futurities Gelding Sweepstakes Champ . N Bar Dot
King Poco Bar
Dubbo Futurities Trail Futurity Champion ....The Equalizer
Lake Cooroibah Versatility Stakes Champ ..N Bar Dot King
Poco Bar
Moonbi Snaffle Bit Trail Futurity Champion .The Equalizer
Moonbi Western Pleasure Futurity Champion................The
Equalizer
Nambour Halter Futurity Champion.......... Discreet O Lena
Nambour Western Pleasure Champion .... The Equalizer
NSWQHA Halter Futurity Champion .... Discreet O Lena
NSWQHA Gelding Stakes Champion N Bar Dot King Poco
Bar
NSWQHA State Champion Reining Horse......... Nonda Tall
Poppy
NSWQHA State Champion Open Cow Horse....Nonda Tall
Poppy
NSWQHA 2YO Trail Futurity Champion.......The Equalizer
NSWQHA Snaffle Bit Trail Champion ....The Equalizer
Premier State Show SB Gelding SweepstakesDead Eye Doc

Claire Donaldson from the NZ Youth Team riding Rusty Frame's bull

'IAN SAVED US FROM MAKING INTERMINABLE MISTAKES AND HE HELPED US SHORTCUT OUR BREEDING PROGRAM AS HE HAD RIDDEN AND KNEW ALL THE HORSES.'
NORMA WHITLEY, FRIEND OF MORE THAN 40 YEARS

'PEOPLE MISINTERPRET WHAT HE TELLS THEM BECAUSE HE IS SO HONEST ABOUT THEIR HORSES' ABILITIES. ALL HE IS DOING IS TRYING TO SAVE THEM TIME, MONEY AND PAIN.'
SUE FRANKS, INSTRUCTOR AND CLIENT

CHAPTER 3 - 'ROCKY' SALE

'IAN ALWAYS SAID THAT ROCKY SALE, WAS THE MOST IMPORTANT SHOW OF THE YEAR. ANY OTHER HORSE SHOW HAS ONLY ONE JUDGE, AT ROCKY YOU HAVE A THOUSAND JUDGES AND THEY'RE ALL WATCHING YOU.'
CLINTON ANDERSON

Between 1978 and 1993 Ian prepared and sold more than three hundred horses through Rockhampton Quarter Horse Sale, earning over one million dollars for his satisfied clients. Year after year his impeccably-trained and superbly-presented horses achieved high top prices and consistently high average prices at a time when sale horses realised only a fraction of what they do today.

The first ever Rockhampton Quarter Horse Sale was held on 9 October 1970 and although it was the first Quarter Horse sale to be held in the area it attracted the biggest crowds on record to Rockhampton's Gracemere saleyards. Twenty crossbred horses were entered, the average price for horses sold was $1030 and the top price of $3000 was paid for a second cross Flapper's Breeze* filly.

Ian made his first appearance at 'Rocky' Sale in 1978 when, as manager of Kolora Stud, he sold three led fillies for a top price of $2200. To put this into perspective, in that same year Jenny and John Kingston paid $7500 for a house in Maryborough, on the banks of the Mary River. The following year, now breaking and preparing horses from his property at Harrami, Ian caused a sensation and changed the whole focus of 'Rocky' Sale when he rode a two-year-old into the ring. In the 1970s few ridden horses of any age went through the sale and it was unheard of for ridden two-year-olds to be offered. Ian's own first cross filly, Kings Charisma, was so calm and worked so well in that terrifying environment that she sold for a whopping $3300 to Mr Fred Christensen of Cooktown and this impeccably-presented filly generated such interest that John and Jenny Kingston of Kolora contracted Ian to sell ridden horses for them each year at the challenging 'Rocky' sale. On selling horses at Gracemere, John Kingston says, 'At 'Rocky' sale you have a maximum of five minutes in a sale ring that is totally unsuitable for selling horses. It is small, hard underfoot and noisy

and young horses put through the ring must be so close to panic but Ian always managed the situation brilliantly. I maintain that for every minute Ian made our horses perform well in the sale ring he added an extra thousand dollars per minute to the price.' Jenny Kingston adds that from 1980 on, whenever the auctioneer announced that Ian was riding into the ring people dropped whatever they were doing and ran to watch the master in action.

By 1980 Rockhampton Sale was recognised as the number one Quarter Horse sale in Australia. It established nationwide selling prices and held most of the Australian sales records.

Jenny Kingston at Rocky Sale.

Horses in the 1980 sale catalogue ranged from the nation's top sprint racing bloodlines to finely-tuned performance horses and well-educated stock horses. Kolora was the most successful vendor in 1980 with the stud's thirteen horses prepared by Ian averaging $2000, significantly higher than the sale average of $1154. Ian achieved the second-top price for ridden mares or fillies when Zannita sold for $4000, and five led Hill King Bars* fillies averaged $2600, double the sale average for that class of sale horse. Once again Ian was widely complimented on his presentation of the Kolora fillies. In the early 1980s two sales were held at Rockhampton each year; one in autumn and the other in November. On 22 May 1981, in spite of low attendance caused by widespread heavy rains, Ian sold the top selling second cross mare, King's Golden Dell, on behalf of Kolora for $2300 and five other Kolora horses for a total average of $1400 against the low sale average of $989.

From the November 1981 sale, Ian's routine for the preparation of sale horses at his property at Widgee was simple, efficient and very effective. Most of the horses he received were unbroken two-year-olds, some were older broken horses and he and his team also prepared many led colts and fillies. The unbroken horses spent only forty-two days with him before the sale; they were rugged, placed under lights, their coats were sweated and they began their education. Each horse had its first two rides in a forty-foot round pen, its second two rides in the reining arena then was ridden along country roads and through Ian's 455-acre property for twenty to forty minutes each day, every day. There were plenty of places to lope circles, stop, back up and turn around to ensure a smooth presentation in the sale ring and Ian says his property looked as though aliens had landed on it because of the training circles scattered everywhere. Lexi adds, 'By the time Ian had finished with them, all the sale horses could hold an almost perfect circle. And no, we did not have a tiny round pen at home the same size as the one at 'Rocky', as so many people thought. Ian's horses worked well in the ring because they were trained properly.' For six weeks the youngsters were

Ian riding Sequence at the 1980 Rocky Sale. Ian prepared and sold 13 horses for an average of $2000 (in today's terms this was the equivalent of the price of a new small car), significantly higher than the overall sale average of $1154.

Lexi Plath hard at work in preparation for the 1989 sale.

worked along creek beds, in the welcome shade of a pine forest and through cattle in open paddocks and by the end of that time they were solid in their foundation and ready for whatever was to be thrown at them during and after the sale. Immediately before the sale all horses were returned to the round pen for a final ride or two with a radio playing loudly to accustom them to the noise they would experience at the sale.

'WE GOT UP, WE WORKED ALL DAY, WE WENT TO SLEEP.'
LEXI PLATH, PAST STABLE MANAGER AND FRIEND, ON THE BUILD-UP TO ROCKY SALE

'ROCKY SALE LOST SOMETHING WHEN IAN STOPPED PUTTING HORSES THROUGH.'
ALLAN WALLACE

'OPPORTUNITIES
ARE NEVER LOST...
SOMEONE ELSE
WILL ALWAYS TAKE
THE ONE YOU
MISSED.'

1983 Mr Versatile preparing a horse that had ringworm in the girth area – Ian rode every sale horse every day, with or without a saddle.

The logistics of preparing large numbers of horses and transporting them to the sale would be daunting to most people, but not to Lexi Plath. She describes years when up to thirty-six sale horses were tied inside the arena while their stables were cleaned. Every horse had to be bathed and shod and in show condition before they departed for the sale in a convoy of vehicles and every horse wore travelling boots and a light rug, all hand-made by Lexi. Preparation of the sale horses did not finish until the moment they entered the sale ring then five minutes later, it was all over.

Ian never had trouble finding staff in the run-up to the sale, there were always young riders wanting sales experience and their time with Ian led many of them into later preparing sale horses for themselves and their own clients. Frank Green recalls the three years he helped Ian prepare for 'Rocky' sale as very tough but says, 'If I had my time over I'd do it again. The only thing I would change is that I would make sure I spent more time with Ian.' Frank tells of days beginning at 2 am and finishing

between 10 pm and midnight. 'Ian never finished until he had ridden every horse that was going to the sale. The other workers would crash on rugs in the alleyway of the stables but I would never weaken until Ian went to bed. I was just a greenhorn when I started and I wanted to learn and one deal he taught me is if you are going to get somewhere you have to put in the hours.' It was not all work; there was plenty of laughter (mostly at Ian's jokes) and lots of fun. One day Frank's two-year-old began bucking for what he thought was no reason. This was not a problem as Frank was a champion rodeo rider but the two-year-old continued to buck and when he looked down Frank noticed a snake moving in the well of his saddle. Frank hates snakes. In fact, he hates them with a passion. The youngster continued to buck, the snake continued to move, Frank used words his mother would not approve of and his so-called friends rolled around the ground laughing. An emergency dismount and a closer inspection revealed that the snake was dead and the joker who had put it there would also have been dead if Frank had got his hands on him.

By the end of 1981 the heavy rain was just a memory and drought conditions prevailed over most of Australia. The November 'Rocky' sale was seen as a severe test of the depth of support for the Quarter Horse industry in Queensland, especially following reports of poor sales in the southern states. However, honours for the sale again went to Ian who presented Kolora's five ridden first and second cross fillies by Hill King Bars* to average $2600 against the sale average of $1227 and he secured the second-highest price of $4000 for first cross mares and fillies for Kolora's young Nina Mia. Ian also sold his own gelding, Kolora Kingsley, for $1700, the third-highest price for a first cross gelding. In June 1982 breeders faced a tough market and 'Rocky' sale reflected this when thirty percent of the horses offered were passed in, the average of the remaining horses sold was only $702 and the auctioneers had to work hard to raise even a $25 bid. Ian topped the sale at $2700 with the purebred Kolora filly, Holly Honey Bar, who was bought by Stuart and Di Jeppeson of Olive Vale, Comet. He also sold the second-top price mare and highest price first cross mare with Kolora's Doc's Zita bought for $1400 by noted Central Highlands horseman, Gordon Salmond Snr of Clermont, and he topped the geldings with two-year-old Poco Chip, bought by Merv Hersom from Gladstone.

Horse sales in NSW and Victoria continued to struggle to find buyers but the November 1982 'Rocky' sale again baffled critics when buyers flocked to pay up to $4000 for horses presented to perfection by Ian. The sale average again was low at $979 but the nine fillies sold by Ian for Kolora averaged an impressive $2567, making Ian and Kolora the top-selling team with the highest sale average. Ian sold the top price and second-top price mares: Pocola at $4000 to Cooktown cattleman, Fred Christensen, and Honey Belle at $3500 to Keith Schottleius of Alton Downs who sent her back to Ian to be trained and shown to further her performance career. Mr D B Sullivan of Springsure paid $3000 for Kolora's palomino filly, Satori, and Mr L Bush of Kennedy in Northern Queensland paid $3000 for another palomino Kolora filly, Petrel.

The drought and the slump in the beef industry during the 1980s meant that many working men with horse skills were lost from the land and graziers found themselves without station hands to break and train their horses. This was where Ian's well-trained, superbly-presented horses became so sought-after. His horses were always started correctly, were presented to perfection and could go straight from the sale yard to muster a paddock or compete in the show ring. In 1983 Ian again turned out an immaculate team. The top selling gelding at $2650 was King's Gold Nugget, sold by D I & B J Siller of Burrum Heads and bought by Peter Eton of Brisbane for polocrosse. Each year at 'Rocky' there was great competition between Ian, Gordon McKinlay and Doug Edgar to sell the highest price horse and 1983 was no exception. Doug Edgar of Armagh Quarter Horse Stud laughingly accused Ian of going to extremes to command attention in the ring when, just as the bidding for Kolora Yolanda reached its

climax and Ian was really working the mare to her utmost, trying to squeeze a few extra dollars from bidders, a girth ring broke and Ian fell off. Yolanda leapt across the ring then immediately turned and trotted back to him for a scratch, showing she was neither intimidated nor frightened. The bidding continued as one comedian called out from the stands, 'Do it again, I missed it!' Kolora Yolanda was the top selling Kolora mare at $4200 and she was bought by D & H McEachern of Dahmac Quarter Horse Stud in Brisbane.

1985 'Rocky' Sale was significant to Ian for several reasons. He presented twenty-six lots for fourteen clients, it was the first year that he prepared and presented a horse for Robert Woodward, the owner of Doc's Spinifex*,

Ian congratulates Ken May from Longreach Pastoral College on his purchase of the $5000 top price horse at 1986 Rocky Sale, Lazy D Sateen, sold by Dee Wink.

Cee Miss Chex, one of 20 horses sold by Ian in 1986. His sale average of $2340 was almost double the overall sale average of $1260.

'WE CAN MAKE
CHOICES IN LIFE.
CHOOSE TO BE THE
BEST YOU CAN BE.'

Ian topped the sale again in 1987 when Kolora Stud's Gold Astral sold for $6500 at what was described as a very depressed sale.

1987 Garrison Stud's Docs Cavalcade.

The 1988 top price horse was Robert Woodward's Docs Alchamy who sold for $8500. This 2yo filly was bought by Bob Conaghan (left) and his son, Phillip, of Barmont Station, Maryborough.

and it was also the year that the mighty little mare, Murrumbo Fiona, went through the Ian Francis stables on her way to the sale and back again to Ian's capable and caring hands to begin her long and outstanding career in working cowhorse, reining and western riding. In 1986 Ian sold twenty horses for ten clients, including the $5000 top-selling horse of the sale, Dee Winks' Lazy D Sateen who was bought on Ian's recommendation by Ken May, horsemanship instructor at Longreach Pastoral College. Ian's average for the 1986 sale was $2340, almost double the sale average of $1260. He again topped the sale in 1987 when Kolora Stud's Gold Astral realised $6500 in what was described as a very depressed market. Under Ian's guidance the seven-year-old Gold Astral had won two reining futurities, was reserve champion at the 1984 Moonbi Working Cowhorse Futurity and was 1984 snaffle bit reining champion. She was bought by the Eskdale West Partnership from Crow's Nest in Queensland. Gold Astral's two-year-old daughter, Kolora Super Nova, also sold at the same sale and was purchased by Clem Richardson of Allandale for $4400. Ian also sold Two Eyed Lucky Bird on behalf of Ken and Cathy Marsh of Quirran-Lea Stud at Gympie and this filly was bought for $5000 by Ken May. Topping the depressed gelding market at $3250 was the Ian Francis-trained Doc's Overcast, a two-year-old by Doc's Spinifex sold by successful Victorian vendor, Robert Woodward of Garrison Stud.

'Rocky' sale received a much-needed boost in 1988 with a sale average almost double the 1987 average and a top price of $8250 for the Ian Francis-trained Docs Alchamy, sold by breeder, Robert Woodward. Docs Alchamy was purchased by Bob and Phillip Conaghan of Barmont Station after a prolonged bidding duel with Emerald horsewoman, Janet Hawkins and the three Doc's Spinifex fillies prepared by Ian for Robert Woodward averaged $6416 against the sale average of $2147. A full sister to Docs Alchamy, Docs Menindee, realised top price at the sale the following year when she sold for $8500 and this two-year-old was again offered by Robert Woodward, prepared and trained by Ian and was bought by the Flohr family of Clermont. 1989 was another year to remember as Ian presented the top price gelding of the sale, top led filly, top broodmare and top-price colt. The top price gelding, Docs Tyson, realised $5200 and was bought by Alan Edgar of Armagh to be used for cutting and general work. Top price colt also went to the Garrison-Ian Francis partnership when another two-year-old, Pines Playboy, was bought by Noela and Steven Booth for $4700 and the Booths also bought the Garrison-bred top broodmare, Docs Analyst, for $3700 and another Garrison mare for $3500. Janet Hawkins, who was the losing bidder for the top price horse the previous year, returned to secure another Garrison-bred Spinifex offering, paying $3200 for Docs Blue Eye. Top led filly was Beavers Cabaletta Doc who was bought by D & A McKay for $3500.

A capacity crowd packed the Gracemere complex on the Thursday night of the 1989 sale to bid on the cream of the ridden horses at a special Starlite Sale. Charlie Flohr, purchaser of the $8500 Docs Menindee, also bought B.S. Mingo's Lucero, the black four-year-old mare who, under Ian's tutelage, was 1989's most successful reining and reined cowhorse futurity champion. She was offered by Henk and Janine Leichsenring of Brisbane and sold for $6500, the second-top price of the Starlite Sale. All up, Ian sold 29 horses at the 1989 sale to gross $101,450 and average $3498 against the sale average of $1968.

Record prices were set at 'Rocky' in 1990 in spite of a continuing depressed rural economy. The Gracemere sale venue was packed out with every seat taken and people standing up to four deep and once again Ian made his presence felt when he sold the top price ridden colt, top led colt, top led filly, top gelding and second-top price mare. The two-year-old top ridden colt, Hug Me Doc, offered by Jenny Kingston's Kolora Quarter Horses, sold for $8000 to Peter and Lesley Bosanquet of Edmonton. Top led colt was the yearling Colinton Beaver who was bought by Keith Holsworth of Emerald for $5250, and the top led filly at $3750 was another yearling, Mint Beaver, bought by Richard Hansen from Alpha. Both

In 1989 Docs Menindee, a full sister to the 1988 top sale horse, topped the sale when she was bought for $8500 by Charlie Flohr of Clermont in Queensland. Charlie also paid $6500 for B.S. Mingo's Lucero at the special Starlite Sale. With Ian in the saddle, the 4YO Lucero had been 1989's most successful reining and reined cow horse futurity champion.

Frank Green breaking in Docs Bob Cat for the 1989 sale. Ian and his team sold 29 horses in 1989 to gross $101,450 and average $3498 against the overall sale average of $1968.

'THERE IS STILL NOT A TRAINER WHO PRESENTS HORSES AT THE ROCKY SALE AS WELL-STARTED AS IAN DID.'
DIANA FRANCIS, CLIENT AND FRIEND

'IAN FRANCIS WAS MY MAN. HE TOOK MY HORSES TO ROCKY EVERY YEAR AND TOPPED THE SALE WITH THEM PRETTY MUCH ALL THE TIME. HE HELPED MAKE DOC'S SPINIFEX THE SUCCESS HE WAS.'
ROBERT WOODWARD, GARRISON STUD

'IF YOU REALLY
WANT TO DO
SOMETHING YOU'LL
FIND A WAY, IF YOU
DON'T, YOU'LL FIND
AN EXCUSE.'

In 1991 Heather Brown's Nonda Undoolya topped the led fillies at $3750 and was bought by the Roberts family of Springsure in Queensland. Ian once more topped the sale in 1991 with the $10,000 Docs Wild Orchid who was bought by Richard Comiskey of Zig Zag Quarter Horse Stud.

yearlings were offered by John and Carol Barton. George Burgess of Dingo in Queensland bought the top-price gelding, Docs Spanna, for $3800, one of twenty-four horses that Ian sold for ten clients to gross $93,900 and average $3980 against the sale average of $2204.

In spite of continuing depressed economic conditions, Ian took centre stage at 'Rocky' again in 1991 following his first win in the NCHA Cutting Futurity. The ten horses he prepared for Robert Woodward averaged a record $5015 with Docs Wild Orchid topping the sale at $10,000. Ian also prepared and presented the top led colt, top led filly and top gelding, selling a total of thirty-two horses for ten clients, grossing $102,250 and averaging $3195 against the sale average of $1925. Docs Wild Orchid, a three-quarter sister to Docs Alchamy who topped the sale in 1988 and Docs Menindee who topped in 1989, was purchased by Richard Comiskey of Zig Zag Quarter Horses who returned the mare to Ian for preparation for coming cutting futurities. The Richard Comiskey-bred and Ian Francis-presented Zig Zag Wandering Star topped the colts at $5500 when sold to Frank Lee of Roma, Heather Brown's Nonda Undoolya topped the led fillies at $3750 and was bought by the Roberts family of Springsure and top gelding, Robert Woodward's Docs Kurrajong, was bought by Bart Phillips of Brisbane for $6500.

Setting a Rockhampton Sale record, the four-year-old Hug Me Doc returned with Ian to the sale ring in 1992 to realise an all-time 'Rocky' high of $16,500. After being trained and shown by Ian in the intervening two years, Hug Me Doc returned to 'Rocky' as NRHA Reining Futurity Reserve Champion, AQHA reining champion and Queensland high point overall performance horse, and he was this time purchased by Lexie Bastable of Mackay. Lexie rang Ian before the sale to ask his advice about buying a yearling colt to raise and show and use later for breeding. 'Ian suggested that buying a yearling might be cheaper in the short term but that it may never go on to do anything and he recommended that I should buy Hug Me Doc.' To Lexie the sale itself was electric. As the bidding for Hug Me Doc slowed Ian threw in another spin and the bidders responded. She had a budget but Lexie's normally reserved friends urged her to make another bid, and another and another and by the time the hammer fell she realised she had spent all the money she had put away for the tax man and had to ring her husband to apologise – but she adds, 'Buying Hug Me Doc was the best thing I have ever done and I never would have done it without Ian.'

Also in 1992 nine Garrison-bred, Ian Francis-trained two-year-olds averaged a record $5311 with Docs Dryanda, top-price mare, being purchased by Richard Comiskey for $10,000. Bush Holdings of North Queensland bought the $6000 top ridden colt, Doc Scobie, and Ian also sold Susie Penfold's $4750 top led colt, Sachem Territorian, who was out of Murrumbo Fiona.

Taking a break at the 1992 Rocky Sale were John Arnold from Longreach Pastoral College, John Osborne of APRA, Ken May and Ian. Ian set an all-time Rocky Sale record in 1992 when Lexie Bastable paid $16,500 for Hug Me Doc, sold by Peter Bosanquet.

Ian ended his connection with 'Rocky' Sale in 1993, going out on another high with a sale record for a mare, top price colt and top and second-top led filly, grossing $123,150 for his clients. Robert Woodward's outstanding Docs Fancy Melody broke the sale record for a mare when she sold for $13,000 to Gina Eddie who had noticed the filly when Ian prepared her for the sale. The three horses offered by Garrison fetched a huge $10,167 average and Alston and Geraldine McKay's Docs Leo Tivio topped the ridden colts and was second-top sale price when Jed Cameron of McKinlay paid $11,500 for him.

Through his attention to detail and his superbly trained and perfectly presented sale horses, Ian raised the standard of what buyers expected when they attended 'Rocky' Sale and he is widely credited with lifting 'Rocky' into its top place amongst annual horse sales in Australia. When his last sale horse had been run through the ring Ian handed over the reins of his sales preparation team to Frank Green, giving Frank his major sale clients. This was a huge boost to Frank's career and has been instrumental in his success today. Frank acknowledges Ian's generosity and says, 'Ian taught me never to rest until the job is done, to leave nothing unfinished and to put 101% in every day. It was incredible to be part of what Ian achieved with his horses.'

Clinton Anderson remembers the six weeks' lead-up to 'Rocky' sale at the Ian Francis Training Stables as, 'The greatest but hardest six weeks of my life. We worked for eighteen hours a day, seven days a week. It was hard but I gained a wealth of experience. Apart from the first two rides in the round pen, every horse was ridden out every day and that is why Ian's sale horses really were broke. They were soft and supple and ready to go to work.' He added, 'Ian always said to me that 'Rocky' Sale was the most important show of the year. Any other horse show has only one judge, at 'Rocky' you have a thousand judges and they're all watching you.' They obviously liked what they saw of Ian Francis.

Relaxing on Great Keppel Island after the 1993 sale were Les Rudd, Les Rudd Jr, Mick Connolly and Ian.

Ian's recollections of 'Rocky' sale

'The first thing that comes to mind when I think about Rocky sale is the enormous effort that Lexi put in every year to see that the horses and I were presented to the highest standard. I got a lot of attention from those sales but, in truth, Lexi deserved many of the accolades for the hours she put in, the workload she carried and for the standards of excellence she set.

I also remember when I ran out of energy and got really sick one year, Raelene Higgins, Frank Green and Glen Wyse dropped what they were doing, packed up their sale horses and took over riding my team until I got myself back together. John Arnold and Gordon Evans offered to take time out from their jobs to help if needed. These people, no matter what, remain forever in credit with me.' Ian Francis

'I WATCHED IAN PUT 36 HORSES THROUGH ROCKY SALE ONE YEAR AND SAID TO MY WIFE, PENNY, IF THERE'S ONE MAN IN AUSTRALIA WHO CAN HELP OUR KIDS, THAT'S THE MAN.'
ALLAN WALLACE

'I ALWAYS HELD IAN IN AWE FOR HOW HE COULD HAVE THOSE LITTLE TWO YEAR-OLDS GOING SO WELL WITHOUT BLOWING THEM UP. THEY HAD GOOD BASICS ON THEM FOR THE LITTLE AMOUNT OF WORK THEY HAD; THEY WERE SOFT, COLLECTED AND VERY CORRECT.'
JOHN ARNOLD, SENIOR SKILLS INSTRUCTOR IN HORSEMANSHIP, LONGREACH PASTORAL COLLEGE

CHAPTER 4 - WORKING COW HORSE

'THE DIFFERENCE BETWEEN THE GOOD ONES AND THE GREAT ONES IS HEART.'

Because of his understanding of cattle and his background in campdrafting Ian believes that the sport of working cow horse was tailor-made for him. Working cow horse was introduced to Australia when the first Quarter Horses arrived in this country and early masters of this demanding event included Greg Lougher and Ian's friend and mentor, Lee Reborse. Training for a cow horse futurity involved training one horse in three distinct disciplines and Ian says it was challenging, intensive and time-consuming but it was also unbelievably exhilarating and very rewarding, especially when he won.

Working cow horse was a marathon event that was held over three days. It consisted of three phases; herd, dry and fence and scores from the three phases were added to determine the winner. Herd work was done along the lines of a cutting contest where a group of cattle was held at one end of the arena; the competitor rode quietly into the herd, selected a beast he thought would best show off his horse's ability, drove it out of the herd and kept it out. Two and a half minutes were allowed for working two or three head of cattle and a horse scored well if it worked on its own, held a line across the arena, neither gave nor gained ground and worked with a smooth, fluid motion showing obvious keenness and interest in the job at hand. Points in herd work were lost for being out of position with the beast, allowing it to return to the herd, for the rider overusing the hand or spur or the horse stirring up the herd or biting or striking the beast.

The dry work was a reining pattern designed to show the depth of the horse's education and its suppleness and response to the rider. A typical pattern featured a figure eight with flying changes followed by a run down the middle of the arena with a sliding stop at the end, one-and-a-half to two-and-

a-half spins, a run back up the arena with the same number of spins in the opposite direction then a run to the middle of the arena with a stop and back-up. A good dry work horse was collected at all times, moved and stopped smoothly, spun correctly and held its head in a natural position without gapping or shaking. A good working cow horse was a versatile horse that could do anything – cutting, reining and day-to-day stock work and if you had a good cow horse, you had a horse with heart and you knew you could take on all comers.

The most thrilling phase of cow horse and the one that drew huge crowds was the fence phase. Fence was what the working cow horse event was all about, it was fast and furious; it could be risky and was often explosive. A single cow was released into the arena for the competitor to work while he demonstrated to the judges that he had complete control of his horse and the beast at all times. The cow was first held on the fence at one end of the arena and then allowed to run three-quarters of the way to the other end to show that the competitor could position his horse anywhere and turn the beast on the fence two or three times each way. The competitor then took the cow to the centre of the arena and circled it once each way. The rider had to be fearless and a successful cow horse had to take control of the cow from the moment it started its run. The horse had to be fast, agile and responsive with a burst of speed and the ability to quickly change gears and leads, stop and turn back. Fence was all about thrills and spills and Ian says, 'I had a few falls, in fact it was not unusual for my horse to fall.' Ian was known for his fearlessness down the fence and was often referred to as a kamikaze pilot. Star Carousel fell with him at the 1986 Moonbi Cow Horse Futurity but he managed to stay in the saddle and the pair won the futurity, the first time an Australian

Photo: Kenyon Sports Photography

Yarranoo Reggae

'IAN HAS A RARE
COMBINATION OF
TALENT, FEEL, TIMING
AND BALANCE THAT
MAKES HIM ONE OF
THE MOST RESPECTED
HORSEMEN IN
AUSTRALIA.'
VIVIAN WEARING,
INSTRUCTOR, MENTOR
AND FRIEND

'NOTHING CAN STOP THE PERSON WITH THE RIGHT MENTAL ATTITUDE FROM ACHIEVING HIS GOALS. NOTHING ON EARTH CAN HELP THE MAN WITH THE WRONG MENTAL ATTITUDE.'

Dan's Lady Cylip, 1985 AQHA Working Cow Horse of the Year & Queensland Hi Point Working Cow Horse of the Year, winner of the Queensland Cow Horse Futurity. Behind Ian is Helen Anning riding the reserve champion.

50

Stock Horse had won the event, and Ian also placed third on D.Bar Paint Your Wagon and fourth with Whisp O'Lena. At the Dubbo Futurity Nonda Tall Poppy fell but this time she emptied Ian out of the saddle. He says, 'I fell off but managed to get back on her before she got up and we won that futurity too.'

Working cow horse was a real crowd-pleaser and always attracted a large audience. Ian says it is remarkable that everyone at a show always came to watch the fence phase but cow horse died in Australia due to lack of support. It was time-consuming for trainers to prepare futurity horses for three events in one for which they couldn't charge extra training fees for the additional work involved and the deep surface used in cutting competition was unsuitable for cow horse. Regional shows always had trouble sourcing cattle and providing facilities for them and trainers also often had difficulty finding suitable cattle. Eventually the dry work section of cow horse evolved into the separate sport of reining and in the late 1980s and early 90s competitors turned away from cow horse and began concentrating on reining. Ian says, 'The people who influenced me most in working cow horse were Lee Reborse, Alan Edgar and Dave Christensen. they had feel, timing and their horses had style.'

DAN'S LADY CYLIP

1985 AQHA High Point Working Cow Horse of the Year

Dan's Lady Cylip was surprisingly small considering her bloodlines and because of her lack of height her breeder, John Arnell, asked Dave Christensen to find her a new home. Ian bought Clip for his client, the late Sel Nichols of N Bar Dot Stud, and the little mare soon won many admirers with her courage and ability. She was reserve champion in the Australian Reined Cow Horse Association Futurity and was Queensland State Champion Snaffle Bit Reined Cow Horse. Ian said, 'She was a good little mare, a real tough little critter and I showed her

Photo: Kenyon Sports Photography

Gold Astral Reserve Champion Moonbi Working Cowhorse Futurity 1984

Photo: Queensland Country Life

Peppy Ann

in cow horse, reining and halter. She ended her career with me as an AQHA Champion, AQHA High Point Working Cow Horse of Australia, and AQHA High Point Reining Horse of Australia with ROMs in halter, reining and cow horse.' Sel Nichols bred two foals from Clip before selling her to the Tapp Brothers from Katherine in the Northern Territory. Her most significant foal was N Bar Dot Touch of Class whom Robbie Hodgeman showed as an NCHA Futurity Finalist and who later became the foundation of Robbie's breeding program. Both Ben and William Tapp won open campdrafts on Clip before she joined their broodmare band. Ian says, 'I guess this proves if you are good enough then you are big enough.'

'I GAVE OUT THE RESULTS OF A WEEKEND SHOW IN VICTORIA OVER TM-WK HOEDOWN ONE TUESDAY NIGHT. IAN AND SOME OF HIS KIDS HAD WON A BUNCH AND I'D PROBABLY REFERRED TO HIM AS THE GREAT AUSTRALIAN ALL-ROUND HORSEMAN. CRUISIN' UP THE NEWELL AROUND MIDNIGHT, IAN TOOK TIME TO LOOK FOR THE LONELY LITTLE LIGHT IN A PHONE BOX (THAT WORKED), STOPPED THE RIG AND CALLED TAMWORTH JUST TO SAY, 'THANKS, MATE!' THAT'S RARE AND IT MEANT A LOT TO ME AT THAT TIME.'
TED HINTZ, SHOW, RODEO AND CUTTING ANNOUNCER OF 40 YEARS

'DON'T PROMISE
ANYTHING YOU
CAN'T DELIVER,
BUT ALWAYS TRY TO
DELIVER A LITTLE
MORE THAN YOU
PROMISED.'

Photo: Kenyon Sports Photography

The kamikaze pilot and the explosive D.Bar Paint Your Wagon 1986

D.BAR PAINT YOUR WAGON

1986 AQHA High Point Working Cow Horse of the Year

1986 QRCHA Cow Horse Futurity Champion

Known as Wags because of his playful personality, D.Bar Paint Your Wagon was a big, strong, colt with not a mean bone in his body. Richard Comiskey bought him at Rocky Sale and sent him to Ian to break and train. Ian said, 'He had the talent and the ability to go to the cutting futurities and, in fact, I did show him in some of the cutting derbies but at the time I was more interested in reining and cow horse so that's the way he went. I really enjoyed training and showing this horse. He was expressive in front of a cow and dynamic down the fence. His one fault was that he would try to be too helpful and sometimes too playful but, in hindsight, I probably showed him too fresh.' Richard Comiskey recalls there was nothing Wags could not handle. At the Gold Coast Cow Horse Futurity Wags drew the one beast that every competitor hoped they wouldn't get,

an aggressive brindle steer that had attitude to burn. Wags handled him well and scored the almost unheard of maximum possible score of 150. Photos of Ian and Wags turning this steer into the fence show how explosive the run was. Richard says, 'Horses like Wags don't come along very often. He had personality and character and was very intelligent. His progeny are smart too.'

MURRUMBO FIONA

1987 QRCHA Cow Horse Futurity Champion

1987 AQHA High Point Working Cow Horse of the Year

1988 QRCHA Cow Horse Derby Champion

Donald Gunn bought two-year-old Murrumbo Fiona at the 1985 NCHA sale and sent her to Ian to be broken in and prepared for the 1985 Rockhampton Sale. Ian fell in love with Fiona as soon as he began working with her, immediately knowing her good mind and athleticism made her more than special. She was a very feminine, willing mare who always gave everything she was asked for and

Ian commented to Jane Penfold, 'I would rather be riding this mare than competing against her.' This led to Jane proposing that her eighty-one-year-old mother should buy only the second horse she had ever owned in her life. Nancy Penfold had rescued a horse from the Toowoomba pound sixty years before and, although working horses were a fact of life on the family property, she had never owned a good working horse of her own. With Jane's help, Nancy arranged for Dave Christensen to bid on Fiona at Rocky Sale. The bid was successful, Fiona returned to Ian for training and showing and the mare stayed with him until she died twenty years later in 2006.

In 1987 Murrumbo Fiona was AQHA High Point Working Cow Horse of the Year. She won the Queensland Reined Cow Horse Futurity and won both the snaffle bit cow horse and snaffle bit reining classes at the AQHA Championships and the Queensland and New South Wales Championships. The following year she was QRCHA Cow Horse Maturity Champion, the SEQQHA Bridle Cow Horse Champion, won the Queensland Reined Cow Horse Derby and again was Queensland and NSW State Champion Working Cow Horse. Ian said of Fiona, 'I never thought she was an enormous athletic talent but she would always try when I asked her to and she always exceeded my expectations. Throughout her career other horses ran big scores that I thought would be hard to beat but I just rode her harder and she always came up and won.' Ian recalls the Moonbi Futurity where the cattle were huge. 'I was circling a bullock that was taller than the mare but she just muscled up and managed him. I later overheard one of the American judges say, "Did you see the guy show that little mare with that huge bullock? That was

Photo: Kanjon Sports Photography

Murrumbo Fiona 1987

'I REMEMBER WATCHING IAN RIDE FIONA AT MOONBI WHEN SHE WAS ONLY TWO-AND-A-HALF. CATTLE WORK WASN'T HER STRONG POINT BUT SHE WAS SO HAPPY; SHE HAD ONE EAR BACK ON IAN AND WORKED ON A LOOSE REIN.'

JANE PENFOLD, PAST EMPLOYEE, CLIENT AND FRIEND

phenomenal!'" Jane Penfold says Fiona was totally relaxed during that run, 'She worked on a loose rein with one ear on Ian and she looked so happy – even though cattle work was never her strong point.'

After what was described as a flawless dry run at the QRCHA Futurity at Pine Lodge that both judges agreed was the best they had seen in a cow horse event, the steer selected for Fiona came into the arena breathing fire, looking as though he would be unmanageable. Judge, Paul Farrell, suggested Ian should be given another beast but on the second judge, Dave Christensen, vetoed that idea, thinking it would be interesting to see what happened. What happened was that Fiona once again managed her beast and won the Futurity. Mrs Penfold was thrilled and her speech at the presentation ceremony brought tears to the eyes of many spectators. She said, 'When you get to your eighties you don't expect a whole new joy in life but that is what I've been given. Where many people wait a lifetime for a winner I've drawn a champion first up. I'm a very lucky woman.' Ian says, 'Murrumbo Fiona taught me that a good-minded horse who would work with me would win more than a great athlete who wants to make some of its own arrangements. She was a real popular horse in her time and one that people would stop what they were doing and come to the arena to see her work.'

VOGUE O'LENA

1988 AQHA High Point Working Cow Horse of the Year

1988 QRCHA Cow Horse Futurity Champion

A record crowd packed the Pine Lodge arena in 1988 to watch the Queensland Reined Cow Horse Futurity for three-year-olds. After a closely-fought battle Ian again won the futurity, aboard Cathy Marsh's Vogue O'Lena. In addition to the Mick Connolly trophy saddle, $2000 prize money and trophy buckle, Vogue O'Lena was the first winner to receive the Nancy Penfold Memorial Trophy, donated by the Penfold family in memory of their late mother who was owner of the previous year's winner, Murrumbo

Ian and Vogue O'Lena, QRCHA Futurity Champion 1988

Fiona. After winning the cow horse futurity, Ian took Vogue back into the arena for the reining futurity which they also won. By this time Cathy Marsh's nerves were almost shot. She says, 'I was always nervous before a big event but Ian would just pat me on the arm and tell me it would be alright – and it always was.' She adds, 'It didn't matter what event he was doing, Ian was always calm and confident before he went into the arena.'

Ian describes Vogue O'Lena as, 'Very cowy and a very talented athlete. She had a beautiful nature, if a little stand-offish and not terribly interested in humans, but was a quality mare who was really built to stay sound and do the cow horse job. She was fancy out of the herd and at any other time I would have gone cutting on her. She handled a snaffle bit well and I felt pretty confident all the way through her training that she was good enough to win cow horse and reining futurities, which she did.' She won three reining futurities in 1988 and was Widgee 3YO Stock Horse Futurity Champion that year, in addition to winning numerous cow horse events. Cathy Marsh says, 'She was a very honest mare, easy to train and her movement was so good she could have gone out and won a hack class. The only time she ever let us down was at Moonbi. She was the favourite for the big cow horse and reining futurities but when she ran into her last stop, something distracted her and I'll never forget the look on Ian's face as she ran sideways!' Not long before the futurity an overseas visitor offered Cathy the enormous sum of $30,000 (remember, this was 1988) for Vogue but Cathy says, 'She was not for sale – then she blew the futurity!'

DONRICA CONCHITA

1989 QRCHA Cow Horse Futurity Champion

Donrica Conchita was a hot, fractious mare who Ian describes as, 'Super, super cowy and phenomenally quick down the fence. She was very expressive in front of a cow and handled her cows very well.' At the 1989 Queensland Reined Cow Horse Futurity Ian had no idea which of his two impressive prospects, Conchita or B.S. Mingo's Lucero, would win; he knew only that both had equal ability and the result would depend on the cattle each drew. Onlookers put their money on the ever-popular Lucero but the day Conchita drew a better cow and won the futurity, leaving Lucero to take out reserve champion.

Donrica Conchita

'IAN WINS BECAUSE HE CAN MAKE THE BEST OF A HORSE'S TALENTS WHILE LEAVING ITS IMPERFECTIONS ALONE.'
DIANA FRANCIS, CLIENT AND FRIEND

'IAN'S THE ONLY TRAINER I KNOW WHO WAS ALWAYS CALM AND CONFIDENT BEFORE EVERY EVENT.'
CATHY MARSH, CLIENT AND FRIEND

B.S. Mingo's Lucero

B.S. MINGO'S LUCERO

1989 AQHA Working Cow Horse of the Year

1989 QRCHA Cow Horse Futurity Reserve
Champion

B.S. Mingo's Lucero was another favourite
in the Ian Francis stable. He was gentle and
a natural athlete and Ian says, 'She was another little mare with a huge heart and she
was an absolute pleasure to train.' Lucero's
owners, Henk and Janine Leichsenring, sent
her to Ian to be broken in when she was two.
Janine says, 'Once Ian got on her she became
a no-go zone – no one else was allowed to
ride her.' Ian remembers the young Lucero
as a natural athlete who had innate cow
sense, a very willing attitude and the potential to excel at the coming cow horse and
reining futurities. After breaking she was
sent home for a spell whereupon she injured
her hind leg so badly that the vet feared
for her life and Janine and Henk doubted
she would ever be ridden again, let alone
compete under saddle. Twelve months later,
sound but badly scarred, Lucero returned
to Ian for some gentle work and two weeks
later they won the Snaffle Bit/Hackamore
Working Cow Horse at the 1988 South East
Queensland Quarter Horse Association
Futurity show. If this was what she could do
after 'two weeks' gentle work and following a twelve month spell, what could she do
if she and Ian decided to get serious? That
question was easily answered. She was 1989
AQHA National Champion Snaffle Bit/

Hackamore Working Cow Horse and at the
1989 QRCHA Cow Horse Futurity she was
neck and neck for Futurity Champion with
Donrica Conchita until she hit a slick spot
in the arena and fell during the fence work
phase. She and Ian quickly picked themselves up, finished their run and still scored
well enough to be sashed reserve champion.
At the last show of her career, the Premier
State Show at Dubbo, she won both the Cow
Horse Futurity and the Reining Futurity
under visiting American judge, Bob Loomis.

NONDA TALL POPPY

1989 R/U AQHA Working Cow Horse of the
Year

1990 QRCHA Cow Horse Futurity
Champion

Her breeder, Heather Brown, describes
Nonda Tall Poppy as 'an exquisitely beautiful mare and a real showgirl.' Tall Poppy
was born on Remembrance Day – the 11th
of the 11th – in 1986. She is tall like her dam,
an athletic Stud Book Thoroughbred mare,
and the Poppy part of her name was chosen
for the day she was born – Poppy Day. Ian
really liked the mare but Heather says, 'Tall
Poppy and Ian were an unlikely match,'
describing them as The Ringer and The
Princess from Graeme Connors' 1996 Bush
Ballad Heritage Song of the same name.
The match between horse and rider may
have been unlikely but it was tremendously
successful. Like her dam, Tall Poppy was
eye-catching and graceful in the ring, even
when she fell over in the Dubbo Cow Horse
Futurity. She was another favourite with Ian
and he said, 'She was a pretty, elegant, man-
ageable mare with presence and I could put
her exactly where I wanted her.' Could he
put her where he wanted her to take out the
QRCHA Futurity for the fifth year in a row
was the question asked in 1990? The answer
was a resounding yes when he rode Tall
Poppy to the futurity win, then backed it up
when he rode Joyce Olsen's Dead Eye Doc to
reserve futurity champion. Tall Poppy also
won the Widgee 2YO Stock Horse Futurity
in 1989, was NSW State Champion Work-

ing Cow Horse and State Champion Reining Horse, she won reining futurities, was AQHA Reining Horse of the Year in 1990 and topped it all by winning four champion classes in one day at the 1990 Brisbane Royal Show. Heather says, 'Ian and Tall Poppy so clearly dominated every class at Brisbane Royal but the highlight was when the judge of the Champion Station Hack class made the mistake of asking Ian to do a freestyle workout. Ian had fun! He did a traditional Stock Horse workout then followed it up with a reining run and finished with classical dressage, doing two-times flying changes as he cantered back towards the judge.' They won.

Photo: Kenyon Sports Photography

Nonda Tall Poppy

'IAN IS AN EXTRAORDINARY MAN AND HE HAS A TREMENDOUS CONNECTION WITH A HORSE; IT COMES FROM THE VERY CORE OF HIS BEING.'
HEATHER PASCOE (NEE BROWN), CLIENT AND FRIEND

'THE REASON WE
DON'T ALWAYS
RECOGNISE
OPPORTUNITY IS
BECAUSE IT
USUALLY COMES
DISGUISED AS
HARD WORK.'

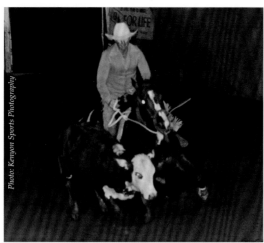

Kolora Double Bar

Mahatma Cote

AQHA WORKING COW HORSE OF THE YEAR

1985   Dan's Lady Cylip

1986   D.Bar Paint Your Wagon

1987   Murrumbo Fiona

1988   Vogue O'Lena

1989   B.S. Mingo's Lucero
        R/U Nonda Tall Poppy

QUEENSLAND REINED COW HORSE FUTURITY (QRCHA) CHAMPIONS

1985   Dan's Lady Cylip

1986   D.Bar Paint Your Wagon

1987   Murrumbo Fiona

1988   Vogue O'Lena

1989   Donrica Conchita
        Reserve - B.S. Mingo's Lucero

1990   Nonda Tall Poppy
        Reserve - Dead Eye Doc

COW HORSE FUTURITIES

1984

Moonbi Cow Horse Futurity Champion .... Gold Astral
NAGS Spectacular Cow Horse Maturity Ch...... Gold Astral

1985

Moonbi Cow Horse Futurity Res Ch.......... Yarranoo Reggae
ARCHA SB Cow Horse Futurity Res Ch .. Dan's Lady Cylip
QQHA Hi Point Cow Horse of the Year ... Dan's Lady Cylip
QRCHA Cow Horse Futurity Champion . Dan's Lady Cylip

1986

Moonbi Cow Horse Futurity Champion .... Star Carousel
Moonbi Cow Horse Futurity 3rd ... D.Bar Paint Your Wagon
Moonbi Cow Horse Futurity 4th .... Whisp O'Lena
QRCHA Cow Horse Futurity Champ .. D.Bar Paint Your Wagon

1987

QRCHA Hackamore Cow Horse Champ ... Kolora Double Bar
QRCHA Hi Point Working Cow Horse .. Kolora Double Bar
QRCHA Cow Horse Futurity Champion . Murrumbo Fiona
QRCHA Cow Horse Futurity 3rd .... Tweed Doc N Wood

1988

Moonbi Cow Horse Futurity Res Ch... Oakey Creek Katie-Jane
QRCHA Cow Horse Futurity Champion .... Vogue O'Lena
NSWQHA Cow Horse Futurity Champion ... Vogue O'Lena
QRCHA Hi Point Cow Horse .... Vogue O'Lena
QRCHA Overall Hi Point Horse .... Vogue O'Lena
QRCHA Maturity Cow Horse Champion Murrumbo Fiona
SEQQHA Bridle Cow Horse Champion ... Murrumbo Fiona

1989

Premier State Show Cow Horse Futurity Ch . B.S. Mingo's Lucero
QRCHA Cow Horse Futurity Champion ... Donrica Conchita
QRCHA Cow Horse Futurity Res Ch.. B.S. Mingo's Lucero
QRCHA Cow Horse Futurity Res Ch...... 3rd Rock the Deck
QQHA State Champion Working Cow Horse Donrica Conchita
QQHA Res State Champ Working Cow H.. B.S. Mingo's Lucero

1990

QRCH&PA Cow Horse Futurity Champ... Nonda Tall Poppy
QRCH&PA Cow Horse Futurity Res Ch .... Dead Eye Doc
NSWQHA State Champion Cow Horse . Nonda Tall Poppy
AQHA R/U Hi Point Cow Horse of the Year .. Nonda Tall Poppy

1992

CQQHA Cow Horse Futurity Champ .... Nonda Music Man
CQQHA Open Cow Horse Stakes Champ .. Nonda Music Man

Demonstrating the art of falling in a cow horse event, Nonda Tall Poppy bites the dust at the Dubbo Futurity. She and Ian recovered to finish the run and win the futurity.

Ian demonstrating working cow horse at a clinic in NZ, riding Pat Robinson's Docs Cheetah

Murrumbo Fiona

'THE MAN DOES HIS HOMEWORK AND THERE ARE NO SHORTCUTS.'
KEN MAY. CLINICIAN AND FRIEND OF MORE THAN THIRTY YEARS

59

CHAPTER 5 - REINING FUTURITIES

'USUALLY WHEN
YOU WATCH A
REINING PATTERN,
YOUR ATTENTION
IS ON THE RIDER.
WHEN IAN COMES
INTO THE ARENA
YOU STOP LOOKING
AT HIM AND
TOTALLY FOCUS
ON THE HORSE.
YOU FORGET IAN IS
EVEN THERE.'
JANE PENFOLD, PAST
EMPLOYEE, CLIENT
AND FRIEND

Nonda Humphrey Oak 1991 QRCHA Reining Classic Champion

*Nonda Music Man 1992 CQQHA Reining
Futurity Reserve Champion*

In the late 1980s and early 1990s reining was the fastest-growing horse sport in Australia. Ian embraced reining but initially his working cow horses did double duty as reining horses and often competed in halter and western riding as well. He started the trend in 1984 with Gold Astral who won both cow horse and reining futurities and she was followed by B.S. Mingo's Lucero, Murrumbo Fiona, Vogue O'Lena, Nonda Tall Poppy, D.Bar Paint Your Wagon, Dan's Lady Cylip and Dead Eye Doc, all of whom were cow horse and reining futurity champions or reserve champions. Rick Tranter was the first Aussie trainer to specialise in reining and he was focussed, successful and seen to be hard to beat. Ian remembers someone saying to Rob Hodgeman that Rick was 'beating Ian Francis with his reiners' whereupon Rob replied that Ian did not have any reiners, all the horses that Ian showed were his working cow horses. He then added, 'The day Ian Francis focuses on reining he will really put his stamp on the event,' and so it proved to be. Ian was the first trainer to win $100,000 in reining competition, he is an NRHA Rider Legend, he trained and campaigned six NRHA Futurity Champions at five NRHA Futurity Shows, won the International Reining Council's IRC World Cup in Canada against international competition and has trained non-pro and open reining horses that have won for their owners and other professional trainers.

Brian and Mary Green's Docs Bob Cat was one of Ian's first dedicated reining horses. He won four reining futurities in 1991 alone and was NRHA high point junior horse and runner up high point reining futurity horse in that year. Lexi Plath says Bob Cat was similar in type and colour to Spindle, another Doc's Spinifex horse that Ian had in training in 1991 and with whom he won the 1991 NCHA Futurity; the only obvious difference between the two was that Doc's Bob Cat is a gelding and Spindle is a mare. Lexi remembers Ian quietly

Amaroos Rock N Return 1992 NRHA Reining Futurity Champion, 1993 & 1994 NRHA Reining Classic/Derby Champion, with owner, Barry Ryan

warming up Bob Cat before a reining futurity with a spin each way and a couple of sliding stops and an onlooker commenting in horror, 'Look what he's doing with his cutting horse! He'll wreck it if he keeps spinning it like that.' To this day Lexi is scathing about that man's inability to tell the difference between a mare and a gelding. Ian often had two or three reiners in his stables at any one time (in addition to his other western performance and stock horses) and they frequently all lined up in the top five at reining futurities – for example, at the 1992 NRHA Futurity Amaroos Rock N Return and Hug Me Doc were Futurity Champion and Reserve Champion – the first time the same trainer had presented the

champion and reserve - and Murrumbo Fiona and Tweed Doc N Wood frequently placed champion and reserve in regional reining futurities.

When looking for a show prospect for a client there are several things that Ian looks for. He says his successful performance horses must have, 'Conformation as it lends itself to performance, structure that lends itself to soundness, bloodlines that have a history of success and temperament or attitude that suggests that the horse will accept training.' He adds that he tries to avoid, 'A deep mouth, thick throat latch, ewe neck, round withers, weak loins, shallow stifle, high or weak hocks, weak pasterns, back at the knee, poor struc-

'HAPPY PEOPLE
DON'T ALWAYS
HAVE THE BEST OF
EVERYTHING. THEY
DO HOWEVER...
MAKE THE BEST OF
EVERYTHING.'

Photo: Kenyon Sports Photography

Hug Me Doc 1992 NRHA Reining Futurity Reserve Champion

Kel Arthur and Ian at the IRC World Cup in 1992. Ian returned to Canada in 1993 where he was IRC Open Division World Reining Champion.

Reeboc Roc 1993 CQQHA Reining Futurity Champion, Thunderbolt Reining Futurity Champion

Photo: Kenyon Sports Photography

1995 NRHA Futurity Reserve Champion, Doc's Leo Tivio, owned by Jed Cameron

Pillamindi Roc 1994 NRHA Reining Futurity Reserve Champion, AQHA runner-up Hi Point Reining Horse of the Year, QRHA Reining Futurity & Reining Derby Champion, Thunderbolt Reining Futurity Champion, SEQRA Reining Futurity Champion

ture of the front legs and hooves too small for the body mass.' On the trainability of any horse, Ian says, 'We can learn some things from observing them but you pretty much have to ride them to see what their retention is like.' Or as John Stanton says, 'You can't tell how far a green frog can jump by just looking at it.'

The mare who epitomised how a reining horse should be built was Murrumbo Fiona. In 1987 the Premier State Show was judged by American reining trainer, Al Dunning. After Fiona won the reining futurity Mr Dunning asked if he could use her as his demo horse at the reining clinic he held at the conclusion of the show. He said of Fiona, 'This is exactly the type of mare we should be using for reining and cow horse – her size and shape make her the perfect reining horse.' Ian nearly didn't enter the reining futurity that day. He says the late Bernard McAneney had been in Queensland to promote the New South Wales Premier State Show; he flattered Ian by telling him how good his horses were and invited him to bring them down to NSW. Ian arrived only an hour before the first go-round of the reining futurity to discover that, as his were late entries, he had to pay a double entry fee. He says, 'I was so disgusted that if they had been my own horses I would have turned around and gone home. As I was showing clients' horses I felt obliged to pay – but I took my revenge by winning the reining futurity plus the open reining and cow horse and then Murrumbo Fiona was the high point snaffle bit horse of the show.'

Fiona's owner, Nancy Penfold, was in hospital and unable to attend the Premier State Show but her daughters, Jane and Susie, were there in her place. Al Dunning had brought a new style of reining saddle to Australia and Jane and Susie, acting as their unsuspecting mother's agents, decided to buy it for Ian but its sale price was more than Fiona's prize money. They struck a deal with Mr Dunning, money changed hands, they presented the saddle to Ian – and told their mother about her generosity when they arrived home. Al Dunning said to Susie, 'There

is no horseman in Australia I'd sooner see using that saddle than Ian Francis.'

Many of today's leading reining trainers worked with Ian when learning their trade. Warren Backhouse says, 'Ian was great to work for but he didn't tell me as much as I'd have liked him to. Now I realise he wanted me to think about things for myself. That really helps me now because when I have a problem with a horse I am able to think it through.' Warren describes Ian's affinity with people, saying 'He has a wonderful rapport with people; he's light-hearted and always cracks jokes and comes up with quotations and little sayings. He has had the biggest influence on me. He's such an icon and if anyone ever had a problem I'd tell them to ask the boss – I've always regarded him as the boss.' Talking about the pressure of being a high-profile trainer in a competitive industry, Warren says, 'We all get down but Ian seems to be able to bring himself out of it. It's hard to relate how he is now with how he had no self confidence when he started.' In a lighter vein, Warren adds, 'He knows he's a bloody awful driver and one time we were heading down the Putti Road on the way to Sydney and there wasn't another vehicle on the road. Ian reckoned they must have known he was coming.'

When asked if he suffers from nerves before a big show, Ian replies, 'Not really, I tried that once and it didn't work. I figure if I get nervous then I'm helping my competitors by giving them an advantage over me.' He adds, 'You lose the edge if you don't have a degree of adrenalin to keep you on your toes but you need to be in control of your emotions. There will always be someone who has a better horse, is better prepared or, these days, who is younger and I don't ever want to give them a head start.' Ian is always ready with a joke, often at his own expense, and does his best to distract other nervous riders with his outrageous sense of humour. He also is renowned for his honesty and fairness. In any reining pattern a competitor is permitted to spin only four times but Ian once miscounted and spun

'WE CALL HIM GOD BECAUSE HE'S SO GOOD.'
VIVIAN WEARING, INSTRUCTOR, MENTOR AND FRIEND

'IF SOMEONE TOLD ME IAN HAD WON A CUTTING OR REINING FUTURITY ON A DONKEY I WOULDN'T BE SURPRISED.'
LEXIE BASTABLE, CLIENT AND FRIEND

'IAN FRANCIS IS ONE OF THE DEEPEST THINKING HORSEMEN I'VE EVER SEEN. HE TAUGHT ME TO THINK MORE.'
WARREN BACKHOUSE, REINING TRAINER, PREVIOUS EMPLOYEE AND FRIEND

'OUR BACKGROUND
AND CIRCUMSTANCES
HAVE INFLUENCED
WHO WE ARE, BUT
WE ARE RESPONSIBLE
FOR WHO WE
BECOME.'

Photo: Kenyon Sports Photography

Amaroos Rock N Return, QRHA Open Reining Champion 1993

five times. He punished himself by crediting the owner's account for the entry fees, travelling expenses and training time, saying, 'The horse's owners had held up their part of the bargain by paying training fees but I had not held up my end of the bargain when I ran an incorrect pattern.' He never repeated that mistake.

The NRHA was formed in 1987 but Ian declined to compete at the early NRHA Futurities which were held half a continent away, in Victoria. He contested his first NRHA Futurity in Dubbo in 1991 and placed fourth with Docs Bob Cat. Before returning home, he and Bob Cat beat the same horses the following weekend at the Premier State Show Reining Futurity and Ian won the Reining Classic with Nonda Humphrey Oak.

AMAROOS ROCK N RETURN

1992 NRHA Futurity Champion

1993 NRHA Derby/Classic Champion

1994 NRHA Derby/Classic Champion

Ian regards Amaroos Rock N Return as one of the best horses he ever trained. He says, 'He was sound and he stayed sound even though he had to work under terrible conditions by today's standards. He had a huge stop on any kind of terrible surface and he could really make the ground move.' Ian took Amaroos Rock N Return and Hug Me Doc to the tough 1992 NRHA Futurity which was judged by Dick Pieper, a respected American trainer and showman. Ian was confident that both his horses were good enough to win the futurity and that it would just be a matter of which

1996 NRHA Futurity Champion, Ayres Roc

one was better on the day. There was little in it, Amaroos Rock N Return was NRHA Futurity Champion with a score of 148½ and Hug Me Doc was Reserve to him on 146½.

Amaroos Rock N Return returned the following year to win the NRHA Classic/Derby, and in that year he also won the QRHA Lyons Motor Inn Super Stakes Open Reining and was AQHA National Champion Junior Reining Derby Horse. The go-rounds of the 1994 NRHA Derby/Classic were closely contested and the open reining featured some very good senior horses. Ian and Amaroos Rock N Return tied for first place in the open but Ian decided not to contest the run-off, preferring to place second and save his horse for the Derby that followed. It was a wise move that paid off when he and the consistently good Amaroos Rock N Return won yet another

run-off to take the NRHA Classic/Derby for the second consecutive year.

AYRES ROC

1996 NRHA Futurity Champion

Ian was not sure he would actually get Ayres Roc to the NRHA Futurity in 1996 as the horse suffered from undiagnosed lameness leading up to the big event. Ian felt that if Ayres Roc was sound he had a chance of making the final but did not actually consider him to be a serious contender for Champion. It would seem that Ayres Roc read Ian's mind and decided to save him the hassle of going through two go-rounds; in the first go-round he tried to back out of a turnaround and the pair came very close to being eliminated but the rest of their run was good enough to get them into the final. Ian worked on Ayres Roc's turna-

'HE'S THE BOSS.'
WARREN BACKHOUSE

'IAN CAN TAKE ANY HORSE AND TURN IT INTO SOMETHING YOU WOULDN'T BELIEVE POSSIBLE.'
ZOË WHARTON, PROTÉGÉ AND FRIEND

'I HAVE WORKED WITH ALL THE TOP AMERICAN TRAINERS; BOB AVILA, TODD CRAWFORD, BOB LOOMIS. WE AUSSIES HAVE A PERCEPTION THAT THE AMERICAN TRAINERS ARE BETTER BUT IN REALITY THEY ARE NOT AT ALL. NONE IS BETTER THAN IAN FRANCIS.'
CLINTON ANDERSON, USA CLINICIAN, PAST EMPLOYEE AND FRIEND

'IF YOU ARE NOT PREPARED TO WRITE IT DOWN AND SIGN IT, YOU PROBABLY SHOULDN'T SAY IT.'

rounds and in the final they tied for the lead with Rob Lawson. They coolly went first in the run-off and dazzled the crowd with a display of deep stops, fast spins and impeccable control, putting the pressure on Rob who spun five times, giving Ian his second NRHA Futurity title.

MAHATMA COTE

1999 NRHA Futurity Champion

Ian bred the buckskin colt, Mahatma Cote, and liked him so much he was tempted to keep him. He describes Mahatma Cote as a real character with a good attitude and says he is a tough horse, mentally, physically and in competition. His owner at the time of the 1999 NRHA Futurity was Annie Wiedon who says, 'He's just a fantastic horse. We expected him to win the futurity final because he had the ability and it felt pretty good when he did win.' Ian again took two very good horses to the NRHA Futurity in 1999, Mahatma Cote

and Bill Bowden's colt, Freckles Gay Doc, who had just won the NSW Reining Futurity. Only fourteen horses were nominated for the NRHA Futurity that year so the committee decided that, instead of a normal go-round to eliminate low-scoring horses, every horse would compete in the final after a dead run where no scores would be recorded. Freckles Gay Doc was the very first horse out for the whole show. After Ian's run, with no warning at any time to any competitor that gear would be checked, a bit gauge that the judge had brought with him from the US was presented and Ian was asked to remove Freckles Gay Doc's bridle. No reining competitor in this country had ever seen a bit gauge before but Ian was confident his gear was correct as it was the same bridle he always used in competition. However, the chin strap was found to be marginally too thin and Ian walked away, knowing he was in trouble. 'Instead of scoring me a zero, they gave me a no-score

1999 NRHA Futurity Champion, Mahatma Cote

2000 NRHA Futurity Co-Champion, Doc Peppa Toy

'HE'S AN INCREDIBLE MAN. ONLY SOMEONE WHO THINKS LIKE IAN DOES COULD MASTER THE THINGS HE'S TAKEN ON. A LOT OF TRAINERS HAVE TRIED A LOT OF THINGS BUT IAN HAS MASTERED THEM ALL.'
WARREN BACKHOUSE

'IAN'S GOT THIS ABILITY TO GET INTO HORSES' MINDS AND WORK THEM OUT PSYCHOLOGICALLY.'
ANNIE WIEDEN, CLIENT AND FRIEND

'IAN COULD PUT A SADDLE ON A CARDBOARD CARTON AND BEAT MOST OF US.'
KEN MAY, MENTOR AND FRIEND

'STUDENTS WHO
PAY THEIR OWN
WAY THROUGH
COLLEGE, RARELY
FAIL.'

*Doc Peppa Toy, Equitana Masters Reining Champion 2001
with Ray Gabbert, Warren Cox, Greg McNamara.*

which disqualified me and effectively gave every other competitor at the show notice to make sure their gear was right. I was not given the same privilege that everyone else received – we should all have been advised about the gear check before the show began. I had to stop the horse's owner from suing the NRHA, but we paid double entry fees to nominate Freckles Gay Doc for the open and I went out and beat all the experienced open horses on a futurity horse.'

DOC PEPPA TOY

2000 NRHA Futurity Co-Champion

2001 NRHA Derby / Classic Champion

NRHA All-time leading money-earner

Warren Backhouse worked for Ian when Doc Peppa Toy came to be broken in. Initially Ian was not interested in her and left her education to Warren but once he had his first ride on the mare he refused to get off. 'She was an awesome mare,' he says. Ray Gabbert knew Ian only by reputation and he says Ian certainly didn't know him but would always say, 'Gidday matey,' whenever they passed each other at a show. Ray recalls, 'One day out of the blue, God rang me. He had a client who was dying of cancer and wanted to find a new owner for this man's good reining mare. I bought Doc Peppa Toy from John Murdock at 11 am and watched her win the 2000 NRHA Futurity that night.' Ray says it was an emotional win especially when an over-

whelmed John Murdock rode the mare into the arena for the presentation. The following year Ian and Doc Peppa Toy won the NRHA Derby / Classic, the Sydney Royal Open Reining Derby and Equitana Asia-Pacific Masters Reining – but only after Ray had bribed Ian with half the prize money to get him to travel all the way to Victoria to compete.

Ray talks about Ian's 'never say die' attitude. At the 2001 QRHA Futurity Show Ian suffered a severe case of food poisoning on the day of the futurity. His friends were so concerned they wanted to take him to hospital but Ian refused, asked Dale Bennett to warm-up his horses, was lifted into the saddle in time to watch Warren Backhouse run a 74 in the Derby, then, last-out, ran 76½ on Peppa Toy – the highest reining score ever achieved in this country. He won the Derby and managed to stay in the saddle long enough to also place fourth in the Futurity on Diana Francis's Most Likely Olena and to have his photo taken before collapsing back into his gooseneck. Ray Gabbert describes Ian as simply the best and a perfect gentleman and says, 'No rider in Australia has accomplished what Ian Francis has accomplished. If it hadn't been for Ian and Peppa Toy I'd be long gone from this sport.'

HUG ME AMBER KING

2000 NRHA Futurity Co-Champion

The 2000 NRHA Futurity was equally as exciting for Lexie Bastable and Rod and Carmel Osborne as it had been for Ray Gabbert. Lexie, who had so much fun at Rocky Sale in 1994 when she successfully bid on the stallion, Hug Me Doc, sent some of Huggie's early foals to Ian to be broken-in. Hug Me Doc had been 1992 NRHA Futurity Reserve Champion and Ian quickly identified that his son, Hug Me Amber King, had the potential to be as good as his dad. Four months before the 2000 NRHA Futurity Ian's friends, Rod and Carmel Osborne, contacted him looking for a non-pro reining horse and Ian recommended that they should consider buying Amber King. Lexie agreed to sell the horse after the futurity – she didn't want to miss out on more excitement in a public place. She says, 'I had never before seen a big reining and I didn't want the show to end. The atmosphere was great and the friendliness and sportsmanship of the competitors was tremendous.' Ian, riding Amber King, tied with himself riding Doc Peppa Toy for first place. Before the run-off he asked all the owners what they wanted him to do. They left the decision to him so he ran a zero on both horses, making them futurity co-champions. Rod Osborne says, 'It was a fairytale result for everyone. It was quite moving and touching and it was wonderful for Ian to prepare and show two champions

– and they were presented immaculately as his horses always are. It was amazing, after the futurity we were the proud owners of an NRHA Futurity Champion.' Carmel Osborne has enjoyed great success as a non-pro and has had an enormous amount of pleasure riding Hug Me Amber King. Carmel and Rod say they have always been good friends with Ian but through Amber King they have also established a great and valued friendship with Lexie Bastable. Ian later recommended another of Hug Me Doc's offspring when Rod was looking for a non-pro futurity horse for himself. He bought Two Eyed Hug as an un-

Hug Me Amber King 2000 NRHA Reining Futurity Co-Champion

'HE LET ME RIDE AMBER KING, WEARING HIS GARLAND OF FLOWERS, OUT OF THE ARENA – IT IS A MOMENT I'LL NEVER FORGET.'
LEXIE BASTABLE, OWNER OF 2000 NRHA FUTURITY CO-CHAMPION, HUG ME AMBER KING

'IF YOU WANT RESULTS YOU GIVE YOUR HORSES TO IAN FRANCIS.'
RAY GABBERT, CLIENT AND FRIEND

'WE HAVE HAD A TREMENDOUS AMOUNT OF SUCCESS AND REWARD BASED ON IAN'S INSTRUCTION AND RECOMMENDATIONS.'
ROD OSBORNE, CLIENT AND FRIEND

'LIVE YOUR LIFE AS
AN EXCLAMATION!
NOT AN
EXPLANATION.'

Photo: Gavin Price

Most Likely Olena 2002 NRHA Reining Futurity Champion

tried three-year-old, sent him to Ian for training and he has enjoyed a huge amount of success with the gelding, the highlight of which was winning the Equitana open reining against open horses and professional trainers when Two Eyed Hug was only four. Rod says, 'I have a huge amount of admiration for Ian and I look on him as being the captain of our industry. His ability is outstanding.'

MOST LIKELY OLENA

2002 NRHA Futurity Champion

After losing her brother and being involved in a horror road accident, Diana Francis (no relation) decided it was time for new adventures. She bought a beautiful two-year-old mare called Kings Miss Olena that Ian was breaking in and says, 'Ian was about the only person who didn't criticise my choice of pedigree.' Ian rode Kings Miss Olena for a few weeks before Diana took her home then, in her futurity year, the filly went back to Ian and in a six week period took out three regional reining futurities and won various halter classes. In a last minute decision, Diana nominated her for the NRHA Futurity where she placed fourth in spite of suffering a leg injury when she was kicked on the trip to Sydney. Some years later, before retiring her to the broodmare band, Diana sent Kings Miss Olena back to Ian to show her in the QRHA Open where she tied for third with Lightning Jack – a great effort for a mare who had not been shown in open reining like her competitors had. Ian says Kings Miss Olena was the easiest horse he ever showed and feels she could have been one of the best if she had been given more opportunities to compete.

Diana bred Kings Miss Olena and her first foal was Most Likely Olena, another horse who had few outings in reining competition. In fact, from the time he was broken in until he contested the 2002 NRHA Futurity, he had only six months work under his girth. Most Likely was started late and suffered minor injuries and a horrendous dose of the flu but Diana says, 'He had a huge heart and the best trainer and I thought he might be in with a chance at the futurity.' She adds, 'I rushed to Widgee to see Most Likely Olena for the last time before he headed to Sydney for the NRHA Futurity, expecting to see much action in his last training run before he jumped on the truck to head south. Ian walked him around the arena for about twenty minutes, spun him several times on each side and stopped him once at each end of the arena. I never said a word because I had full faith that Ian would get the best out of the horse in the time given.' She continues, 'The bold little colt strode on the truck early the next morning as if he had the futurity bagged. However, Ian kept my expectations realistic by phone from Sydney when he said two other trainers had horses that were so broke it was scary.' Diana could not be in Sydney to see Most Likely compete and she was working right up until the time Ian rang at 11 pm to tell her of their win. She says, 'I can't describe the elation I felt – I howled for about an hour and a half and my feet didn't touch the ground for days. I had worked so hard for so long to get this colt to the futurity and it felt so good to win.'

The 2002 NRHA Futurity win was Ian's last competitive reining ride. Most Likely Olena was his sixth NRHA Futurity Champion and, during his victory lap of the arena, Ian decided it was time to quit reining and concentrate on conducting clinics, property development and training cutters. He says, 'I had no unfinished business in reining, I'd won futurities, derbies and everything in between and I decided to walk away while I was on top.' After a second victory lap in which he hammed it up, Ian stepped off and called it quits. As Diana says, 'What a great note to retire from reining on.'

Some time later Ian borrowed Most Likely Olena to demonstrate the sport of reining at Equitana Asia-Pacific. Diana says Ian was thrilled when he stepped up on the colt, months after having last ridden him. 'He spun and stopped him briefly like there was no tomorrow to test Most Likely's retention. Ian was beaming as the colt passed with flying colours – the trainer had also passed with flying colours.' Soon after Equitana Diana sold Most Likely Olena to Germany where, after a lengthy break in quarantine, he continued to compete very successfully. When talking about Ian, Diana says, 'He is such

'IAN WON SYDNEY ROYAL REINING FUTURITY ON MOST LIKELY OLENA – AND REMEMBERED TO LET ME KNOW A WEEK LATER.'
DIANA FRANCIS, CLIENT AND FRIEND

'IAN HAS A WONDERFUL RAPPORT WITH PEOPLE, THE SAME AS HE HAS WITH HIS HORSES.'
WARREN BACKHOUSE

'AFTER THE 2002 NRHA FUTURITY I REMEMBER BARELY BEING ABLE TO CONTACT IAN FOR ABOUT SIX MONTHS AS EVERYONE WANTED SOME OF HIS TIME.'
DIANA FRANCIS, OWNER OF MOST LIKELY OLENA, 2002 NRHA FUTURITY CHAMPION

'WHY WOULD YOU FLY ME ALL THE WAY TO AUSTRALIA TO CONDUCT A CLINIC WHEN IAN IS ALREADY THERE?'
CRAIG JOHNSON, US REINING TRAINER

'BITE OFF MORE
THAN YOU CAN
CHEW! YOUR
MOUTH IS
PROBABLY BIGGER
THAN YOU THINK.'

Riverholme Royal Oak 1997 NRHA Reining Futurity Reserve Champion with Raelene Higgins and owners, Vicki and Bruce Neville

an all-rounder and he has given so much value to everyone in the industry. Yes, he is a showman when he needs to be and I think it would be interesting to compare him with the Parellis and the whisperers of this world, to see how many of their horses appear in top performance line-ups the way Ian's horses do.'

2006   NRHA Rider Legend   Ian Francis

When Ian retired from reining after winning the 2002 NRHA Futurity, he had won more reining futurities and was the highest money-earning trainer with earnings of $125,000, more than double the earnings of the second-highest money earning trainer who was on only $62,000.

'Two people had the most influence on me in reining. Firstly, Lee Reborse in the 70s inspired me with his feel and finesse. Later, Raelene Higgins helped me elevate my horses from snaffle bit to bridle class horses and helped me to refine what I was doing with my feet. Raelene has a remarkable amount of instinct and insight in her horsemanship and can quickly and accurately pinpoint factors that limit performance. She doesn't spend a lot of time worrying about it if her observations offend you, either!' Ian Francis

NRHA REINING FUTURITIES

1992
NRHA Futurity Champion .... Amaroos Rock N Return
NRHA Futurity Reserve Champion .... Hug Me Doc

1993
NRHA Derby / Classic Champion. Amaroos Rock N Return

1994
NRHA Futurity Reserve Champion .... Pillamindi Roc
NRHA Derby / Classic Champion... Amaroos Rock N Return

1995
NRHA Futurity Reserve Champion .... Doc's Leo Tivio

1996
NRHA Futurity Champion .... Ayres Roc
NRHA Derby / Classic Champion .... Doc's Leo Tivio

1997
NRHA Futurity Reserve Champion .Riverholme Royal Oak

1999
NRHA Futurity Champion .... Mahatma Cote

2000
NRHA Futurity Co-Champion .... Doc Peppa Toy
NRHA Futurity Co-Champion .... Hug Me Amber King

2001
NRHA Derby / Classic Champion .... Doc Peppa Toy

2002
NRHA Futurity Champion .... Most Likely O'Lena
NRHA All-time leading money-earner .... Doc Peppa Toy

2006
NRHA Rider Legend .... Ian Francis

AQHA HI POINT REINING HORSE OF THE YEAR

1985   Dan's Lady Cylip

1987   Murrumbo Fiona

1988   R/U Vogue O'Lena

1990   Nonda Tall Poppy

1994   R/U Pillamindi Roc

REINING FUTURITIES

1983
Nambour Reining Futurity Champion .... Gold Astral
Nambour Reining Futurity Reserve Champ ..... Honey Belle

1984
SEQPHC Reining Futurity Champion .... Gold Astral
SEQPHC Reining Futurity Reserve Champ ...... Honey Belle
SQQHA Reining Futurity Champion .... Gold Astral
SEQQHA Reining Maturity Champion .... Gold Astral

1985
Moonbi Reining Futurity Reserve Champion ..Dan's Lady Cylip
Nambour Reining Futurity Champion .... Dead Eye Doc
Nambour Reining Futurity Res Champ ...D.Bar Paint Your Wagon
Nambour SB Reining Futurity Champion .... Star Carousel
SEQPHC Reining Futurity Champion .... Peppy Ann

SEQQHA Reining Futurity Champion .....Dan's Lady Cylip
SQQHA Reining Futurity Champion........Dan's Lady Cylip
AQHA Hi Point Reining Horse..................Dan's Lady Cylip

1986
Nambour Reining Futurity Champion ..... Murrumbo Fiona
SEQPHC Reining Futurity champion ...... Murrumbo Fiona

1987
Moonbi Reining Futurity Champion .... Murrumbo Fiona
Moonbi Reining Futurity Reserve Champ . Tweed Doc N Wood
Premier State Show Reining Futurity Champ ...Murrumbo Fiona
Kenilworth Reining Futurity Champion .. Murrumbo Fiona
QRCHA Reining Futurity Champion ... Kaylen Silver Threads

1988
NEQHA Frances Anderson Memorial
Open Reining Champion .... Murrumbo Fiona
QRCHA Nancy Penfold Memorial
Reining Futurity Champion ....Vogue O'Lena
SQQHA Reining Futurity Champion..............Vogue O'Lena
Premier State Show Reining Futurity Champ .. Vogue O'Lena
QRCHA Hi Point Reining Horse ....Vogue O'Lena
SEQQHA Bridle Reining Champion .... Murrumbo Fiona
SEQQHA Reining Futurity Champion .... Rock the Deck

1989
Premier State Show Reining Futurity Champ .B.S. Mingo's Lucero
SQQHA Reining Futurity Champion... B.S. Mingo's Lucero
QRCHA Reining Futurity Res Champ. B.S. Mingo's Lucero

1990
QRCHA Reining Futurity Champion ..... Nonda Tall Poppy
NSWQHA Reining Futurity Champion..........Vogue O'Lena
NSWQHA State Champ Reining Horse.. Nonda Tall Poppy
Garden City Supastock Reining Futurity Ch ..Nonda Tall Poppy
AQHA Hi Point Reining Horse of the Year.. Nonda Tall Poppy
Premier State Show Reining Futurity Champ . Docs Bob Cat

1991
NRHA Hi Point Junior Horse...........................Docs Bob Cat
NRHA R/U Hi Point Futurity Horse ....Docs Bob Cat
NRHA Trainer's Award.. Ian Francis
QRCH&PA Reining Futurity Champion .... Docs Bob Cat
QRCH&PA Reining Classic Champ Nonda Humphrey Oak
Garden City Stakes Reining Futurity Champ . Docs Bob Cat
Toowoomba Reining Futurity Champion .... Docs Bob Cat
Toowoomba Reining Futurity Res Ch.. Nonda Humphrey Oak
Premier State Show Reining Futurity Champ .. Docs Bob Cat
Premier State Show Reining Classic Ch..Nonda Humphrey Oak
SEQQHA Reining Futurity Champ..Amaroos Rock N Return

1992
QRHA Reining Futurity Champion .... Reeboc Roc
QRHA Open Reining Champion .. Amaroos Rock N Return
CQQHA Reining Futurity Champion .... Hug Me Doc
CQQHA Reining Futurity Res Champ Amaroos Rock N Return
CQRHA Reining Futurity Champ Amaroos Rock N Return
CQRHA Reining Futurity Res Champ....Nonda Music Man
QRCH&PA Reining Classic Champ .Amaroos Rock N Return
SEQQHA Reining Futurity Champion .... Hug Me Doc
Thunderbolt Reining Futurity Champ Amaroos Rock N Return
Thunderbolt Reining Futurity Res Champ ...... Hug Me Doc

1993
QRHA Reining Futurity Res Champ..Amaroos Rock N Return
QRHA Winter Classic Reserve Champion .... Reeboc Roc
Cattle City Reining Futurity Champion Mexican Sundance
Cattle City Reining Futurity Res Champion ...... Reeboc Roc
QRCHA Lyons Motor Inn Open Reining Amaroos Rock N Return
International Reining Council World Cup Champ .Ian Francis
CQQHA Reining Futurity Champion................. Reeboc Roc
QRCH&PA Open Reining Champion ....
Thunderbolt Reining Futurity Champion .... Reeboc Roc

1994
QRHA Spring Classic Reining Champion..... Authentic Roc
Cattle City Reining Futurity Champion . King's Miss O'Lena
SEQRHA Reining Futurity Champion.. King's Miss O'Lena
CQQHA Reining Futurity Champion ... King's Miss O'Lena
QRHA Joyce Olsen Memorial Reining
Futurity Champion ....Pillamindi Roc
QRHA Reining Derby Champion...................Pillamindi Roc
SQQHA Reining Futurity Champ Amaroos Rock N Return
Thunderbolt Reining Futurity Champion .....Pillamindi Roc
SEQRA Reining Futurity Champion ....Pillamindi Roc

1995
NEQHA Frances Anderson Memorial
Reining Futurity Champion ....Doc's Gold Dude
QRHA Joyce Olsen Memorial Reining
Futurity Champion .... Doc's Leo Tivio
QRHA Joyce Olsen Memorial Reining
Futurity Reserve Champion ....Doc's Gold Dude
QRHA Reining Derby Champion...................Pillamindi Roc
QRHA Reining Derby Reserve Champion.... Authentic Roc

1996
NRHA Open Reining Champion .... Doc's Leo Tivio
NEQHA Frances Anderson Memorial
Reining Futurity Champion ....Ayres Roc
QRHA Open Reining Champion .... Doc's Leo Tivio
QRHA Derby Reining Reserve Champion.. Doc's Leo Tivio
NSWQHA Reining Futurity Champion....... Doc's Leo Tivio
QRCHA Reining Futurity Res Champ Amaroos Rock N Return

1997
Nambour Reining Spectacular Champion
NSWQHA Reining Futurity Champ Riverholme Royal Oak
QRHA Joyce Olsen Memorial Reining
Futurity Reserve Champion ....Riverholme Royal Oak
QRHA Jackpot Reining Champion...Riverholme Royal Oak
QRHA Jackpot Reining Reserve Champ ... Sachem Sandfire

1998
QRHA Pacific Rim Securities Futurity Champ Sachem Lillipilli
Sydney Royal Reining Futurity Champion Sachem Lillipilli

1999
QRHA Open Futurity Champion ....Sachem Lillipilli
NSW Reining Futurity Champion.............Freckles Gay Doc
Qld Open Western Show Futurity Champ .. Freckles Gay Doc

2001
Sydney Royal Open Reining Derby Champ .Docs Peppa Toy
Equitana Masters Reining Champion .... Ian Francis
QRHA Open Derby Champion................... Docs Peppa Toy

2002   VRHA Open Derby Champion

CHAPTER 6 - STOCKMAN'S CHALLENGES AND STOCK HORSE FUTURITIES

'DO NOT FOLLOW WHERE THE PATH MAY LEAD. GO INSTEAD WHERE THERE IS NO PATH AND LEAVE A TRAIL.'

Nonda Military March

Photo: Kenyon Sports Photography

Nonda Nightbird & Yarranoo Reggae at the 1984 Australian Stock Horse Championships at Dalby

The Australian working horse industry was forced to change when the cattle industry was gripped by a severe depression in the 1970s. During these hard times large cattle stations and outback properties laid off thousands of experienced stockmen, men with years of experience working cattle who had spent thousands of hours breaking and working station horses. When these men were forced to leave the land their horse-handling skills left with them. When the beef industry recovered, properties became more family-oriented and family members and contract musterers became the new stockmen and women of the bush. Instead of riding for days to find cattle, these new stockmen trucked their working horses in and out of remote areas and began using helicopters to muster – but there were no well-broken and educated young stock horses to replace

working horses as they aged and retired.

Heather Brown wanted to establish a memorial to her late father, Reg, by introducing an annual challenge between Australian stockmen that would encourage the education of young Australian Stock Horses, advance the Australian Stock Horse industry and encourage the use of new working bloodlines. She called on her friend, Ian Francis, to use his knowledge of horses and cattle and his experience of competing in and winning all types of working horse events to design a truly Australian working horse competition. Ian took the western reined cow horse event, put an Aussie spin on it, combined it with the traditional sport of campdrafting and created what has become the greatest competition for working horses in Australia - The Cloncurry Stockman's Challenge, otherwise known as the Melbourne Cup of the Bush or the Olympics of the Outback. Ian designed a two-phase event, combining a 'dry' phase based on a simple reining pattern with a second 'wet' phase of working a beast around a set course, to test each horse in every aspect of its training and ability. Ian's rationale was also to encourage stockmen to learn how to put a solid, basic foundation on their young horses, to train them correctly and to make those young Stock Horses marketable into the more advanced Australian sports of polocrosse and campdrafting.

Heather based her Stockman's Challenge in her father's old stamping ground, the tiny town of Cloncurry in north-west Queensland. Cloncurry was founded in 1867 and soon boomed to become the biggest and most boisterous town in outback Queensland. Set amongst rocky hills and creeks, gidgee trees and buffel grass, 'The Curry' is said to breathe cattle and have copper and gold in its veins. Aboriginal people lived and worked there for generations and fought wars with pastoralists and prospectors.

In 1916 Cloncurry was the main source of Australia's copper and the town is justifiably proud of being the birthplace of the Royal Flying Doctor Service. Heather Brown designed a magnificent $20,000 perpetual trophy – The Reg Brown Memorial Cup which is based on a stockman's 'quart pot', a fast-boiling pot with companion drinking mug - donated it to the Cloncurry Show Society and the Cloncurry Stockman's Challenge, open to all breeds and all sexes of horses younger than six years old that were bred above the Tropic of Capricorn, was launched at the 1984 Cloncurry Show. In later years entries were restricted to horses four years and under, bred anywhere in Australia, registered with a breed society or not. Heather says, 'The Cloncurry Stockman's Challenge is not for a privileged few, it is for all horses including station-bred horses. One of the joys has been to see horses with a touch of Percheron or Brumby enter The Challenge which is now one of the most popular events at the annual Cloncurry Show.'

1987 Cloncurry Stockman's Challenge Champion & highest-scoring Australian Stock Horse, Star Carousel, with Ian and owner, Heather Brown

STAR CAROUSEL

1987 Cloncurry Stockman's Challenge Champion

Ian's response to people who asked why he had not previously entered the event he designed was simple, he says, 'I would not travel that distance to compete until I knew I was mounted and prepared well enough to win.' It is only fitting that a Heather Brown-owned and Ian Francis-trained horse should win the first Cloncurry Stockman's Challenge that he ever contested. Heather bought the Australian Stock Horse, Star Carousel, as a short yearling. She says the filly was aloof and not at all interested in people but Heather was impressed with her mind and her ability to focus on the job at hand. Star Carousel was broken in by Ian and the pair formed a bond that you occasionally read about but rarely see. 'They had a marriage,' says Heather, 'and she always gave him one hundred and fifty percent.' Ian says he always found Star Carousel to be good-minded and trainable, 'I set out showing her in reining, working cow horse and working

Star Carousel at the 1987 Cloncurry Stockman's Challenge

After winning the 1987 Cloncurry Stockman's Challenge, Jane Penfold and Star Carousel became bogged on the road between Cloncurry and Longreach

'HE'S GOT EDUCATED HANDS AND EDUCATED FEET.'
TERRY HALL

'A LOT OF HIGH PROFILE TRAINERS HAVE BEEN HELPED INTO THEIR CAREERS BY IAN, INCLUDING ME. HE HAS BEEN A BIG HELP TO ME WITH MY CHALLENGE HORSES.'
JOHN ARNOLD

'FOR EVERY PERSON
THAT CLIMBS THE
LADDER TO
SUCCESS... THERE
ARE TEN STILL
WAITING FOR THE
ELEVATOR TO SHOW
UP.'

1996 Cloncurry Stockman's Challenge Champion, Docs Gold Dude

stock horse events with the long range plan to take her to Cloncurry Stockman's Challenge as a four-year-old. She was reserve champion at the Australian Reined Cow Horse Futurity and Champion at the Moonbi Cow Horse Futurity in her three-year-old year.' There was much interest in Star Carousel at the 1987 Cloncurry Stockman's Challenge because of Heather's association with the area and her desire to win the event was well known.

Ian rode Star Carousel through almost faultless rounds to win the title twelve points ahead of the nearest of their forty-four rivals, scoring 336 points out of a possible 400 and winning the grand sum of $2161. After the excitement and the photos were over, Heather says she watched as Ian put Star Carousel into a yard then wandered off to get himself an ice cream. 'Star Carousel kept her eyes on Ian as he walked away and disappeared into the crowd. She just stared into that crowd until he reappeared and as soon as she saw him again she whinnied and whinnied – to me, that's what having a horse is all about.' Heather retired Star Carousel to the broodmare band after her Challenge win and the mare has never had a saddle on her again to this day.

DOCS GOLD DUDE

1996 Cloncurry Stockman's Challenge Champion

In 1996 Ian rode away with his second Cloncurry Stockman's Challenge Cup and the more respectable winner's cheque of $10,000, this time on the four-year-old palomino stallion, Docs Gold Dude, owned by West Australian, Barry Ryan. Again Ian won by a huge margin of ten points, this time against sixty-eight ringers and other professional trainers. However, a number of the losing competitors complained that his pretty palomino with the flowing blonde mane and tail was not butch enough to win an outback challenge but Ian just shrugged and smiled. After all, he and Docs Gold Dude had worked consistently throughout the challenge to win both the dry and wet phases in the first go-round and they went into the final as the favourite against ten other horse and rider combinations. Second in the 1996 Challenge was young Stewart Wallace who, some time before, had spent three months working with Ian and breaking in horses for him. When Stewart bought his Challenge horse he asked Ian if he thought they had a chance in the event and Ian replied that the horse had the ability and should do well if Stewart trained him correctly. Stewart followed Ian's advice to the letter and was rewarded by placing reserve champion to his mentor. In a nice twist, Stewart's mount, Docs Holly Oak, is a full brother to Ian's mount, Docs Gold Dude.

In 1996 the committee felt that horses were being entered into the Cloncurry Stockman's Challenge that were not the correct age so they decreed that all nominated horses would be mouthed to ensure they were four years or under. Ian took two horses on the 1650 kilometre, twenty-two-hour trip to Cloncurry in 1996. His second horse was Spinnies Wrangler, a colt he had known as a yearling and therefore was confident he was only four. Although he was the right age and his papers confirmed it, unfortunately Spinnies Wrangler's teeth

Whisp O'Lena, 1986 Widgee 3YO Stock Horse Futurity Champion and Hi Point 3YO

said otherwise and he was eliminated from the Challenge. Ian disputed this ruling which was upheld but the furore that resulted over this decision caused the rules to be changed in subsequent years. Once again, Ian did not send the disqualified horse's owner a bill.

WIDGEE STOCK HORSE FUTURITIES

Widgee is barely a dot on the map of Queensland but the district became famous in the horse world in the 1980s firstly as the home of Ian Francis Training Stables and then for another of Ian's innovations, the Widgee Stock Horse Futurities. In 1984 Ian and his friends John and Jeanette Elliot and Anne Sutherland put their heads together to come up with a series of futurities to provide young stock horses with an opportunity to compete under conditions less demanding than those generally available. Ian says, 'John and Jeanette were tireless workers and promoters of Australian Stock Horses and they wanted to see the Widgee area promoted and become known as a centre for Stock Horse activity.' Jeanette Elliot says, 'Ian and John were far-sighted enough to know what the Stock Horse industry needed and Anne Sutherland contributed some very good ideas.' John and Jeanette ran the Widgee Futurities until John's death and Jeanette's move from the area in 2002, by which time Jeanette says, 'The Widgee Futurities had become the most important event on the Stock Horse calendar.'

'HE'S WON EVERYTHING BAR THE MELBOURNE CUP.'
NORM STAG

'IF YOU WANT IAN TO WIN SOMETHING JUST TELL HIM HE CAN'T.'
KEN MAY, CLINICIAN AND FRIEND FOR MORE THAN THIRTY YEARS

'HE'S VERY FOCUSSED BUT HE ALWAYS HAS TIME FOR YOU AND NEVER FORGETS PEOPLE. WE ALWAYS KNEW WE COULD CALL ON HIM.'
NORMA WHITLEY, FRIEND OF MORE THAN 40 YEARS

'THE SECRET TO
SUCCESS, IS HOW
YOU DEAL WITH
FAILURE.'

Stock Horse Futurities were a new concept in the Australian working stock horse world. The Widgee Futurities were designed for riders and trainers to give a solid foundation to their young registered Australian Stock Horses so those young horses could then move into, and be more competitive in, traditional stock horse contests such as campdrafting, polocrosse and working stock horse classes. Back in the 1980s the only market that existed for Australian Stock Horses was for mature ridden horses, four years and over. There was no money for young horses and Ian saw that extra benefits of the Widgee Stock Horse Futurities would be to provide a market to sell young stock horses and generate recognition for sires and dams. The first Widgee Futurity was held in July 1985, and it has been held every year since then includes futurities for two-year-olds and three-year-

olds and a maturity event for four-year-olds. The Widgee Futurities include a halter class for each age, the two-year-old ridden futurity takes the form of a hack-style workout with simple changes and, at the judge's discretion, the horse may be required to open and close a gate, ground-tie, carry a sack of cans or similar objects and accept the rider cracking a whip from its back. Three-year-old futurity horses work a more challenging stock horse pattern and are required to work a beast similar to the western working cow horse event, and four-year-old maturity horses combine a working pattern and work a beast on similar lines to a campdraft course.

Ian won his first Widgee Futurity in 1986 on Cathy Marsh's athletic mare, Whisp O'Lena. Ian describes Whispy as, 'Kinda hot but electric on a cow.' Cathy Marsh

Nonda Tall Poppy, 1990 Brisbane Royal. Champion Station Hack, Champion Stock Horse Under Saddle, Champion ASH Mare or Gelding Under Saddle, owned by Heather Brown.

says her mare was, 'An awesome little cow horse. She blew the socks off them when she handled the beast because she was so intent.' Whisp and Ian had a brief but profitable partnership, not only winning the Widgee Futurity but also a snaffle bit reining futurity, Stock Horse under saddle and champion Stock Horse classes and they placed in cow horse futurities. Two years later, in 1988, Ian again won the Widgee 3YO Futurity on another of Cathy Marsh's Roc 'O'Lena daughters, the gorgeous Vogue O'Lena. Cathy says, 'Vogue did well in the halter and dry run but she excelled in the mini cow horse section. She placed high in all phases and won overall.'

Australian Stock Horse breeder, Cyril Bidgood, sent three good stock horses to Ian from 1989 to 1991. Ian says, 'Cyril was a good client and I showed some real nice horses for him.' The first of these nice horses was Havenville Gentle Abbey who won the 4YO Futurity in 1989 in spite of falling on slippery ground when working his beast. The same year, Havenville Sally Ann ran reserve champion to Ian and Nonda Tall Poppy in the 2YO Futurity and was set to return the following year to contest the 3YO Futurity but snapped a fetlock. Ian says, 'It was a shame because she was a very able filly, very elegant and she had plenty of breeding.' In 1990 Ian again won the 3YO Futurity, this time on the very cowy Havenville Crackshot. Ian says, 'Crackshot was a very good yard horse and could really travel with a cow.'

Ian is the only trainer to win every division in the Widgee Stock Horse Futurities and the later Monto Stock Horse Futurities. In 1989 he took out eight places at Widgee, including the overall high point horse. However, Jeanette Elliot says, 'There was only one stock horse competitor who had him bluffed and that was John Elliot, only because John was more determined than Ian.' Ian's response is, 'Once John set his mind on something he was tough to bend.'

Whisp O'Lena, 1986 Widgee 3YO Stock Horse Futurity Champion with Ian and owner, Cathy Marsh

BRISBANE ROYAL STOCK HORSE

1983
Champion Station Hack .... Nonda Native Whimsey

1984
Champion Station Hack .... Nonda Nightbird

1990
Champion Station Hack .... Nonda Tall Poppy
Champion Ridden Stock Horse........... Nonda Tall Poppy
Champ ASH Mare/Gelding Under Saddle.. Nonda Tall Poppy
Champion ASH Under Saddle .... Nonda Tall Poppy

CLONCURRY STOCKMAN'S CHALLENGE

1987
Challenge Champion .... Star Carousel
Highest-scoring Australian Stock Horse ....Star Carousel
Reg Brown Memorial Cup .... Star Carousel

1996
Challenge Champion .... Doc's Gold Dude
Elder Statesman Cup .... Ian Francis

STOCK HORSE FUTURITIES

1986
Widgee 3YO Futurity Champion .... Whisp O'Lena

1988
Widgee 3YO Futurity Champion .... Vogue O'Lena

1989
Widgee 2YO Futurity Champion .... Nonda Tall Poppy
Widgee 2YO Futurity Reserve Champ....Havenville Sally Ann
Widgee 3YO Futurity Champion ....Donrica Conchita
Widgee 4YO Futurity Champ...... Havenville Gentle Abbey
Widgee Futurities Overall Hi Point.... Nonda Tall Poppy

1990
Widgee 3YO Futurity Champion .. Havenville Crackshot
Widgee 3YO Futurity Reserve Champion ....Dead Eye Doc

1991
Monto 2YO Futurity Champion......... Nonda Music Man
Monto 3YO Futurity Champion. Nonda Humphrey Oak
Monto 4YO Futurity Champion.... Havenville Crackshot
Widgee 2YO Futurity Reserve Champ.. Nonda Music Man

'HE'S A TOP GUY, A GREAT, GENUINE BLOKE.'
CYRIL BIDGOOD

'I WAS THERE, IN THE BOX, AT THE 'CURRY'. I HEARD THE MUTTERINGS ABOUT THE PRETTY PALOMINO 'BARBIE DOLL' COLT – 'HELL, HE'S EVEN LEFT HIS MANE ON!' THEY SAID. BUT I'LL NEVER FORGET THE IMPROMPTU CLOWNING ACT IAN TURNED ON WITH RUSTY FRAME AND SPEC THE CLYDESDALE WHILE THE COMMITTEE DOUBLE-CHECKED THE SCORES. THE SPINS AND SLIDES AND TURNS LEFT NO DOUBT THAT THE MAN WHO ESTABLISHED THE CHALLENGE HAD A BIT MORE UP HIS SLEEVE IF HE NEEDED IT. THE OLD CLYDESDALE DIDN'T GO TOO BAD EITHER.'
TED HINTZ, SHOW, RODEO AND CUTTING COMMENTATOR OF MORE THAN 40 YEARS AND FRIEND

CHAPTER 7 - CUTTING FUTURITIES

'DON'T LET
ANYONE'S OPINION
DESTROY YOUR
BELIEF IN
YOURSELF.'

Ian was inducted into the NCHA Hall of Fame at the 2007 NCHA Futurity. He has trained and ridden three NCHA Futurity Champions, two Reserve Champions and one NCHA Derby Champion and as Phil Webb said, 'On the basis of the number of horses shown at NCHA Futurities to the dollars he has won, he's ahead of everyone.'

Ian describes himself first and foremost as a cattleman rather than a horseman, and his lifetime experience of working with cattle gives him an unfair advantage in the cutting pen. His understanding of how cattle think and his ability to predict how they will react gives him an edge that few other cutters can ever hope to attain. Most people in the cutting industry probably do not realise that Ian's other job of conducting clinics throughout Australasia, New Caledonia and the United States takes him away from home for many weeks each year so his futurity horses actually get significantly less work than other trainers' horses. However, he agists feedlot cattle so has a continuous supply of fresh cows for his futurity prospects to work and his young horses work a cow – not a bag – almost every day that he is at home.

The cutting horse evolved in the United States in the early 1800s when there were few fences and thousands of cattle grazed vast areas in the south west of this newly-colonised country. Cattlemen gathered large herds on open plains and individual cows had to be separated or 'cut' from the herd for branding, to be sent to market or moved to new sections of grazing land. It was soon discovered that the job could be performed easily and efficiently by using specially bred and trained horses called 'cutting horses'. The Australian National Cutting Horse Association was formed in 1972 and cutting in this country has become a highly competitive sport.

Photo: Dave Christensen

Total focus & concentration at the start of Ian's successful 2003 NCHA Futurity run on One Hellofa Spin

Ian cut his first cow in 1971 and he dabbled in cutting over the years, mostly on the versatile Kings Gold, with Beryl playing the part of the 'cow' during early practice runs. He won his first cutting competition in the early 1980s on Eternal Slave who had previously been trained and shown by Bill Bassett, however, his main interest in the 70s and 80s was campdrafting and cow horse and he had his hands and stables full with horses for those disciplines.

Ian's serious interest in cutting was sparked the first time he rode the two-year-old Spindle on a cow and it was a revelation to him. In 1991, after he and Spindle won the NCHA

Futurity, Ian was addicted and began looking for another horse on which he could repeat the win. He prepared two Doc's Spinifex mares, Docs Wild Orchid and Docs Desert Rose, for the 1991 Rocky Sale. His client, Richard Comiskey, wanted a good cutting mare and after a bidding duel with another of Ian's clients, Stephen King who happened to be Spindle's owner, Richard paid the top sale price of $10,000 for Docs Wild Orchid and sent her back to Ian to be trained for the NCHA Futurity. Stephen King bought Docs Desert Rose and also returned her to Ian and at the 1993 NCHA Futurity Ian made the final on both mares. Stephen King says, 'Desert Rose was only a little mare, about 14hh and the cattle in the finals were bigger than her. They were tough cattle and they frightened a lot of the futurity horses. I was sitting in the front row when Docs Desert Rose was Futurity Reserve Champion, half a point behind the winner. She was awesome.' Both Desert Rose and Wild Orchid went home to their respective owners who continued to show them and soon after Richard Comiskey rang Ian from Tamworth to tell him that the two mares had tied and were co-champions of the NCHA Gold Cup. 'How good is it for horses he had trained to go on and do that with other riders?' Richard asks. He says, 'You can

waste years trying to train horses that have no ability but Ian taught me how to feel if my horses have ability or not. He taught me all I know about cutting and I remember trying to pass on some tips to other competitors but they rubbished me and said I didn't know what I was talking about. Years later those same guys tried to teach me the same tips!' He adds, 'People didn't understand how Ian's horses worked. What they didn't realise is that his horses have so much confidence because he puts such a great foundation on them. If they get out of position he doesn't panic and they don't panic, he knows he can just get them back where they belong.'

In 2000 Ian imported the two-year-old Smart Chic Olena colt, Chic Chexer. He says, 'From his first foal crop of only twenty foals Chic Chexer produced the reserve champion NCHA Snaffle Bit Futurity and finalists in the NCHA open and non-pro futurity and campdraft winners. Chic Chexer himself won the Goondiwindi Cutting Derby and finalled in the Toowoomba Derby and even though I had to geld him because of his declining fertility he proved he had the capacity to be a sire. It is a good feeling to know I selected a horse that has made a contribution and that my judgement on the horse and his breeding is vindicated.'

'IF THAT DUDE TURNS UP, HE'S READY.'
GRAHAM LAMEY

'HE'S ALWAYS GLAD TO SEE YOU.'
RICHARD COMISKEY, CLIENT AND FRIEND

'IAN IS PROBABLY THE MOST CAPABLE HORSEMAN WE HAVE EVER HAD ANYTHING TO DO WITH. IF WE HAD DECIDED TO GO CAMPDRAFTING INSTEAD OF CUTTING I'M SURE IAN WOULD HAVE WON THE WARWICK GOLD CUP FOR US.'
STEPHEN KING, CLIENT AND FRIEND

Eternal Slave 1981

'BEING A
COMPETITOR IS
LIKE BEING A
TURTLE... YOU
DON'T GET
ANYWHERE IF YOU
DON'T STICK YOUR
NECK OUT.'

Photo: Kenyon Sports Photography

1991 NCHA Cutting Futurity Champion, Spindle

SPINDLE

1991
NCHA Futurity Champion
NCHA Futurity Limited Division Champion

Spindle was just born to cut a cow and Ian says there was nothing else in the world that she could do better. Originally Ian bought her sight unseen as a reining prospect for his client, Stephen King, after talking to her breaker who really liked her. 'I asked about her legs and he said that one front leg was a bit offset. Well, her leg was more than a bit offset and I was bitterly disappointed that I hadn't checked more thoroughly as I am particular about straight legs.' Ian thought Spindle had no chance of staying sound in reining so he put her on a cow and was amazed by her perfect instinct right from the start. He says, 'She is still the most powerful two-year-old I have ever worked, so much so that I had to check

her papers to make sure she wasn't a three-year-old. She was a real independent sort of mare and if I got after her for something she could get pretty snorty.' Lexi Plath describes Spindle as very suspicious and says she and Ian were the only people who could catch her. Lexi says, 'Her leg was bad and she probably would have broken down with another trainer but Ian was very patient with her. He didn't have to work her down, he knew he only had to saddle her up, trot her in a circle then take her into the arena where she would latch onto a cow straight away.' Ian kept Spindle sound by careful shoeing and light work. She was easy to train and Ian thought she had a real chance in the futurity but he kept quiet about her until late in the year when he needed reassurance and asked David Hogg to check her out and tell him he was right about her, which David did. However, 'Before long word got out that this reining and reined cow

Goondiwindi Derby Champion, Ian's own Chic Chexer

horse bloke had a really good futurity prospect and what a waste it was because reining
trainers don't win cutting futurities and he'll
never handle the pressure.' Ian was amazed
at this reaction, particularly after having been
a professional trainer in high pressure events
for twenty years. 'I had never heard of myself
being thought of as suspect under pressure. I
let it get under my skin and it provided great
motivation to make sure I did the job right at
the futurity.' He adds, 'If they had treated me
nicely I probably would have been happy just
to make the final but they offended me and
that was all I needed to go all out to win.'

After what Ian describes as an average first
go-round, he and Spindle won the second go-
round. 'I rang Stephen King and told him we
were in the final and asked if he was going
to come down to watch. Spindle was his first
cutting horse and he didn't have a clue what

I was talking about – he didn't think it was
very interesting.' In typical Ian fashion, whenever Stephen had made his weekly call to ask
how Spindle's training was progressing, Ian
told him, 'On yeah, she's going alright,' so
Stephen and Sue figured there was little point
in trekking all the way to Tamworth, instead
they spent the weekend with their kids at a
gymkhana. However, the morning after the
futurity Stephen says, 'I woke up and said
to Sue, we won the futurity last night – there
were no mobile phones back then so no one
had told me but Ian rang about half an hour
later and said I was $27,000 richer.' Stephen
very generously gave Ian half his prize money as a bonus and, the following year when
Docs Desert Rose was NCHA Futurity Reserve Champion, he gave Ian and Lexi tickets
to travel to the USA.

Ian says he made a mistake with his time

'I BELIEVE IAN IS THE
BEST HORSEMAN IN
THE COUNTRY AND
HE IS UNEQUALLED AS
FAR AS TRAINING
FUTURITY HORSES
GOES.'
RAELENE HIGGINS

'IF HE WASN'T A
TRAINER HE'D STILL
BE AN AMAZING PER-
SON AND IF HE LIVED
AND WORKED IN THE
USA WE WOULDN'T
BE ABLE TO GET NEAR
HIM FOR HIS FANS.'
JENNY BROWN, PAST
EMPLOYEE, CLIENT AND
FRIEND

Photo: Kenyon Sports Photos

Mahatma Cote the only horse to show in both the NCHA and NRHA Futurities. He was NRHA Reining Futurity Champion in 1999 and missed the NCHA Cutting Futurity final by only one point.

Roc Me Gently, full sister to Mahatma Cote.

management in the final and quit his second cow too soon, 'I left the gate open for someone else to beat me but no one was good enough to get through.' Ian and Spindle won by a comfortable margin of one-and-a-half points, and then won the Limited Division of the Futurity, but that was still not enough to silence Ian's critics. 'They said I wasn't much of a cutting horse trainer and I was just lucky to have such a good mare. This was a bit disappointing and I said as much to William Tapp. He told me that if I got too disappointed I should just take that winner's cheque out of my pocket and look at it and I would feel a hell of a lot better. Smart fella, that William.' Ian's success with Spindle was the motivation he needed to take cutting seriously and so he began looking for future futurity prospects.

ONE HELLOFA SPIN

2003
NCHA Futurity Champion

2004
NCHA Derby Champion

Raelene Higgins told Ian that one day she would breed a foal from her mare, Rocs Stardust, that he would win the NCHA Futurity on. She was right. When Ian and Raelene witnessed the birth of One Hellofa Spin Ian says, 'Raelene crept down the paddock to check the foal then moved some distance away and did a little dance so I figured she had a filly.' On the way back to the house Ian suggested, with his tongue firmly in his cheek, that he could probably get Raelene good money for a foal bred like that, and says, 'If we were to print her reply we would have to sell this book under the counter.' He adds, 'Raelene is good at naming foals and she believes that names are important.' Raelene agrees and says, 'It was apparent to me from the day she was born that she was special and there was no doubt in my mind that she would win the NCHA Futurity. She had to have a special name and it took me a long time to come up with the right one.' Raelene started One Hellofa Spin under saddle then sent her to Ian to be trained for the futurity. She says, 'Ian's feel for horses, his understanding of how their minds work and his ability to read cattle, combined with his strength and knowing when not to use his strength makes him the best horseman in the country. He tries to take every horse to the highest level he can and he does it for every horse that he trains. He was the best man for the job.'

Ian says, 'One Hellofa Spin got to me a bit late after sustaining a minor injury but she started on a cow brilliantly and stayed like that all the way through.' Raelene had high expectations of the little mare she called Zoë but she restrained herself for two weeks before ringing Ian to ask about her progress. Ian replied, 'She's great but she's real quick off her ends' and Raelene said, "That's good, it makes two of you!"' After another two months he commented to her, 'I don't think 80 points is go-

Photo: Dave Christensen

One Hellofa Spin 2003 NCHA Cutting Futurity Champion

'WHEN HE GETS A
HORSE TRAINED, IT
STAYS TRAINED FOR A
LONG TIME.'
PHIL WEBB, TRAINER

'IAN IS THE MOST
VERSATILE HORSEMAN
THAT THIS COUNTRY
– AND THE WORLD
– HAS EVER SEEN.'
KEN MAY, CLINICIAN
AND FRIEND OF MORE
THAN THIRTY YEARS

'YOU'D THINK THEY'D
LEARN NOT TO PISS
HIM OFF.'
RAELENE HIGGINS

'IT MAKES NO DIFFERENCE WHICH WAY THE WIND IS BLOWING, IF THE SAILOR DOESN'T KNOW WHERE HE IS GOING.'

Photo: GMP Events

ing to be enough,' suggesting she was so good someone would have to add extra points to the score sheet. Zoë's training was interrupted for seven weeks when a horse fell on Ian and broke his leg and a rib and by the time she arrived at the futurity she had only spent seven and a half months on cattle. However, Ian says, 'I felt really confident of her ability, so much so that I put Raelene up on her in the Non Pro Futurity. Raelene really didn't want to ride her because she had only sat on her in front of a cow for less than a minute and felt she might jeopardise her chances in the open.' Ian had confidence in them both and they placed in the non pro final, even though Raelene had not shown as a non pro all year and got on Zoë at the gate without even any preparation in the practice pen.

Ian says, 'People had seen Zoë at a few pre-works and there was a fair bit of talk about her before the futurity. By the time we got through the second go-round she had a fan club bigger than Elton John's.' Dave Christensen asked Ian how he felt about the final and Ian replied that Zoë would handle anything he put in front of her. They drew last in the first herd and as Ian watched the herd settle he thought there should be enough fresh cattle left when his turn came. The stands were packed with spectators and he says, 'When I rode into the herd I have never experienced a crowd so quiet, you could have heard a pin drop. It was kind of eerie.' When Ian put Zoë on her first cow 'She was electric and I have never heard a crowd give the kind of support they gave to her. On my last cut I heard Robbie Hodgeman in the corner tell me I had ten seconds to go. I had a few cattle still out front and one red steer that I really didn't want – but he stepped out to the front and I knew that if I waited for him to clear I wouldn't have time to cut another one so I went with him. I heard later that Raelene almost passed out there and then.' The crowd made so much noise that Ian did not hear the buzzer so he stayed on the steer until he heard show commentator, Ted Hintz, speaking. 'Ted is too professional to talk while the run is on so I quit. I nearly wound my neck off turning to check the clock and, boy, I was relieved

Dick Smith arrived at the Widgee property in his chopper to visit his daughter, Jenny Brown, who worked for Ian for six months.

Jenny Brown & 2004 NCHA Derby/Classic Champion, Docs Spinafrec, said, 'Without Ian there's not a chance I'd ever have come close to winning the NCHA Derby. It was one of the most exciting moments of my life.'

to see it was stopped.' Raelene was numb as she watched Zoë and Ian win the futurity and she says, 'It didn't hit home until the video arrived. It was a life-long dream come true.'

Ian is reluctant to talk about something that happened about two months before the futurity, for fear of sounding foolish. 'I was asleep at home and I awoke about 2 am with the strangest feeling that I have never had before or since. I knew with absolute certainty that One Hellofa Spin would win the NCHA Futurity. Now, I have not had a lot to do with religion and I doubt that God is a cutting fan and even if he was I expect he would be far too busy to be interested in the Australian Futurity, but if I was religious I would think that God spoke to me that night.'

Ian and One Hellofa Spin returned in 2004 for the NCHA Derby where they tied for cham-

'MOST OF THE SO-CALLED CUTTING EXPERTS DIDN'T EXPECT THE QUIET QUARTER HORSE SHOWMAN/REINER TO SLIDE IN AND TAKE THEIR FUTURITY MONEY ON SPINDLE AND THERE WAS NO WAY HE COULD GET ANOTHER ONE ON THE CUTE LITTLE MARE IN 2003 – WRONG! DARCY AND JANET TWOHILL TOOK THE ODDS AND PROVED THEM WRONG AGAIN WITH GIDGEE COALS. HOW GOOD WAS THAT?'
TED HINTZ, SHOW, RODEO AND CUTTING COMMENTATOR OF MORE THAN 40 YEARS AND FRIEND

'COMPETITION
DOESN'T CREATE
CHARACTER - IT
EXPOSES IT.'

Photo: GMP Events

Gidgee Coals, 2005 NCHA Cutting Futurity Champion

pion in the final with Todd Graham. Todd ran-off first and had a really good run. Raelene says, 'As soon as Todd waved his hat in the air I silently thanked him because I knew it would piss Ian off and make him more determined to beat him.' Right up until Ian and Zoë worked their last cow it was anybody's final but that last cow gave them enough points to win the Derby. Ian says, 'There has been a lot written about One Hellofa Spin and I expect there is more to come, but for my part few people get to ride a Phar Lap, a Makybe Diva, Smart Little Lena or a One Hellofa Spin. Raelene allowed me the privilege of training and showing one of the all-time greats and for that I am forever grateful. One Hellofa Spin – Futurity Champion, Triple Crown Champion, NCHA All-time Money-earner – she's simply the best.'

GIDGEE COALS

2005
NCHA Futurity Champion

Ian has broken in horses for Janet Twohill for the past thirty years. She says, 'It seems as though I've had horses with him forever and I think I hold the record for the highest number of horses that he's sacked.' Ian replies that, after so many years and so many average horses, he really wanted to win a big futurity for Janet. Before she married, Janet says she tried very hard to buy a mare by Docs Spinifex but as a single parent she could never afford one. When she married Darcy Twohill her circumstances changed and she was able to send two mares to Spinifex, one of the resulting foals was the big, strong but emotionally fragile Gidgee Coals. Ian says, 'Gidgee Coals showed a lot of cow and physical ability but she had a busy mind and was always anxious, aware of what was going on around her and was easily distracted. It took judgement and discipline not to scare her but I felt that if I gained her confidence that she would be a good one.' About three months before the NCHA Futurity Dave Christensen asked Ian what he had and Ian replied, 'Nothing that I can win on.' Dave thought Ian was being canny and not giving anything away but Ian was honestly not confident that the mare would come good. Janet says, 'She was a hard mare for Ian to train and I wasn't excited about going to the futurity when the best he would say was "Yeah, alright" when I asked how she was going.' Two months before the futurity Gidgee began to gain confidence and Ian says, 'By show time I was pretty optimistic about her chances.'

As always, the atmosphere at the NCHA Futurity was amazing and Ian's reaction at the end of his run said it all – raising his fist in the air he knew he had it won. Janet was on crutches after breaking her leg but she says, 'Even with only one leg I nearly jumped over the fence when we knew Ian and Gidgee Coals had won.' Ian says, 'Showing a big-time winner for Janet and Darcy had been one of my goals for a long time. Janet has been a very good friend and supporter and I have ridden quite a few of her horses and Darcy has given me a lot of help in recent years and it was great to see them enjoy their win.' He adds, '2005 was a tough year for me personally and I really had to challenge myself to get up and go again. Training and showing Gidgee to that level helped answer some questions about heart and commitment that I had about myself.' Janet concludes, 'Ian was really choked up at the presentation. He is a wonderful human being. We have been friends for so long and have seen each other through some big highs and terrible lows; he's the best friend I've got in the world.'

Gidgee Coals, 2005 NCHA Cutting Futurity Champion with her owners Janet and Darcy Twohill (second and third from left)

'Of all the photos I have of Gidgee Coals, this one says so much. In spite of his demeanour, I know Ian is pleased too.' Janet Twohill, owner of 2005 NCHA Futurity Champion, Gidgee Coals.

Robyn Priest's Hickaboonsmal

'YOU HAVEN'T LOST
UNTIL... YOU STOP
TRYING.'

Tassa Chic 5th place 2000 NCHA Futurity

Photo: GMP Events
Jenny Brown, with Ian at the NCHA Futurity

*'I watched Graham Amos show Freckles
Bohemia at Moonbi and her style and
presence really impressed me. I also saw a
lot of Chilla Seeney and Mr Jessie James.
Todd Graham has had such an impressive
career and I've tried to learn something
from watching him show. Rob Hodgeman
and David Hogg have been a big help and
the way that Dave trained and showed
Doc's Town Crier to NCHA Futurity
Champion has a lot to do with my style
today. Raelene Higgins has had a fair bit
to do with my success at futurity level;
she provided the encouragement to win the
first, the means to win the second and the
motivation to win the third.' Ian Francis*

CUTTING

1991	NCHA Futurity Champion Spindle
	NCHA Limited Futurity Champion Spindle
1993	NCHA Futurity Reserve Champion Docs Desert Rose
	NCHA Futurity Finalist Docs Wild Orchid
1999	NCHA Futurity Reserve Champion Oak's Melody
2002	NCHA Derby Finalist Roc Me Gently
2003	NCHA Futurity Champion One Hellofa Spin
2004	NCHA Derby Champion One Hellofa Spin
2005	NCHA Futurity Champion Gidgee Coals
2006	NCHA Futurity 3rd place Dixie Chic O'Lena
1991	Moonbi Cutting Futurity Reserve Champ Spindle
1992	SEQQHA Open Cutting Spindle
	Comet Cutting Futurity Reserve Champion Pretty Good Doc
	Rockhampton Futurity Reserve Champion Pretty Good Doc
	CQQHA Futurity Reserve Champion Pretty Good Doc
2002	Cotton Country Derby Champion Chic Chexer
2005	Comet Cutting Futurity Champion Gidgee Coals
	Victorian Cutting Futurity Champion Gidgee Coals
2006	Cotton Country Futurity Reserve Champion Gidgee Coals
	NCHA Futurity Finalists Acres Spinafrec & Lethal Warrior
	NCHA Derby Finalists Gidgee Coals & Dixie Chic O'Lena
	Darling Downs Cutting Club Champion Rider Ian Francis

Dixie Chic O'Lena

'IT IS A FEATHER IN IAN'S CAP TO HAVE WON THREE NCHA FUTURITIES. TO WIN ONCE IS GREAT BUT TO WIN THREE TIMES IS THE ULTIMATE.'
ROBERT WOODWARD, GARRISON STUD

'IAN FRANCIS HAS MORE FEEL FOR A HORSE THAN ANYONE I'VE EVER SEEN.'
ROBERT WOODWARD, GARRISON STUD

CHAPTER 8 - CLINICS

'IF YOU KEEP
DOING WHAT
YOU'RE DOING,
YOU'LL KEEP
GETTING WHAT
YOU'RE GETTING.'

'Explanation, demonstration, imitation, repetition, repetition, repetition.' Ian Francis

Ian has conducted sell-out schools and clinics throughout Australia, New Zealand, Fiji, New Caledonia and the USA since 1980. His aim at these clinics is to give riders the tools to produce happier horses, thus improving the horse industry in general. Ian's clinics have ranged from basic horse handling to advanced horsemanship, horse breaking, campdrafting, reining, cutting, trail, halter and working cow horse.

Ian is a master at the art of communication and he can communicate in a way that is easy for his students to understand. He has a wonderful ability to teach riders how to develop the foundation on which to build and improve their riding and training, whether they are in

the dressage arena, the cutting pen or at pony club. He instils confidence and helps riders to be more effective and efficient in the saddle, shows his students how to overcome resistance and unwanted behaviour in their horses and to know when to allow the horse to relax and think about what it has learned.

Ian has a unique ability to break down each manoeuvre into simple step-by-step exercises and drums into his students that, 'You must understand the mechanics of each manoeuvre before you can fix what is wrong.' He teaches students to practise each step until it becomes a second nature and only then to focus on the next step until it, too, is habit. Students then learn to tie one step to the next until each ma-

You have to understand the mechanics before you can fix what is wrong

'HE'S A PERFECTIONIST. HE KNOWS IF HIS HORSE'S FOOT IS SIX INCHES OUT OF PLACE BECAUSE HE HAS THE FEEL.'
NORM STAG

'YEARS AFTER ATTENDING HIS CLINICS, WE STILL USE DIFFERENT THINGS THAT WE PICKED UP FROM IAN. EVERYONE WHO WENT TO HIS CLINICS GOT SOME-THING OUT OF THEM.'
PAT ROBINSON, NZ

'IAN FRANCIS IS THE MOST UNDER-UTILISED RESOURCE IN AUSTRALIA.'
PETER BAILLIEU

'IAN CAN HELP SUCH A WIDE VARIETY OF RIDERS. BECAUSE HE HAS SUCH A VERY GOOD COMMAND OF THE BASICS IT DOESN'T MATTER WHAT LEVEL YOU AND YOUR HORSE ARE, HE CAN ADAPT TO SUIT.'
JOHN ARNOLD, SENIOR SKILLS INSTRUCTOR IN HORSEMANSHIP AT LONGREACH PASTORAL COLLEGE, MENTOR AND FRIEND OF OVER 20 YEARS

'WHO IS RIGHT IS
NOT IMPORTANR.
TRY AND FIGURE
OUT WHAT IS
RIGHT.'

Moura Clinic 1980

Relaxed horses and focussed riders at a Fernvale clinic in November 2006

It's all about timing your responses...

noeuvre flows and is polished to perfection. He encourages by saying, 'If you get 1% improvement each day, in 100 days you will be perfect.' He teaches how to control the individual parts of the horse and explains how each part affects the others – what may appear to be a problem in the hind end may actually originate somewhere else. Ian tells the bad with the good. If a horse does not suit the rider's ambitions for it he will tell the rider to either change the horse or try another discipline.

Ian emphasises that everything you do with your horse now must relate to what you do later on. He shows how to create a desired reaction from a horse, how to know what is correct and what is not and how to react and reward the slightest improvement. He says, 'Timing is critical, get the timing wrong and you end up punishing rather than rewarding your horse for doing the right thing. If a horse has a lot of problems with one specific move, give a lot of short-term rewards. By knowing when the horse is doing the best it can the rider can achieve the lightness he wants.' Ian encourages students to do as little as possible and as much as necessary to get the results they want with their horses and he emphasises that for communication with a horse to be successful it must be understood. Students attend Ian's clinics to improve their riding skills and overcome problems and they leave with an improved understanding of how and why the things they do affect their horses. Most of all they go away with an improved relationship with their horses.

John Kingston says, 'Ian has gone from being nervous about talking in public to being one of the best communicators I've ever come across.' John recalls in the late 70s Ian was asked to give a talk to the local Pony Club to explain to the children how to look after their horses. 'He came to me and said he couldn't do it so I wrote out what I thought he should say and Ian did the presentation. The next time he was asked to do something similar, I wrote half, Ian wrote half then presented it. Now his presentations are very factual and smooth and interspersed with lighter moments. He can sit on a horse, making it do things and you would